Indigenous Resistance and Development in Winnipeg: 1960–2000

ARP Books (Arbeiter Ring Publishing)
205-70 Arthur Street
Winnipeg, Manitoba
Treaty 1 Territory and Historic Métis Nation Homeland Canada R3B 1G7
arpbooks.org

Cover design by Bret Parenteau
Interior layout by Relish New Brand Experience.
Printed and bound in Canada by Imprimerie Gauvin on certified FSC ® paper.
Second printing, December 2023

Canada Council for the Arts | Conseil des arts du Canada
MANITOBA ARTS COUNCIL | CONSEIL DES ARTS DU MANITOBA

Canada
Manitoba

ARP Books acknowledges the generous support of the Manitoba Arts Council and the Canada Council for the Arts for our publishing program. We acknowledge the financial support of the Government of Canada and the Province of Manitoba through the Book Publishing Tax Credit and the Book Publisher Marketing Assistance Program of Manitoba Culture, Heritage, and Tourism.

MRA MANITOBA RESEARCH ALLIANCE
CCPA 25 CANADIAN CENTRE for POLICY ALTERNATIVES MANITOBA OFFICE

Social Sciences and Humanities Research Council of Canada | Conseil de recherches en sciences humaines du Canada
Canada

We are pleased to acknowledge the financial support of the Social Science and Humanities Research Council of Canada through the Manitoba Research Alliance's Partnership Grant *Community-Driven Solutions to Poverty: Challenges and Possibilities.*

LIBRARY AND ARCHIVES CANADA CATALOGUING IN PUBLICATION

Title: Indigenous resistance and development in Winnipeg : 1960-2000 / Shauna MacKinnon and Kathy Mallett, eds.
Names: MacKinnon, Shauna, editor. | Mallett, Kathy, editor.
Description: Includes bibliographical references.
Identifiers: Canadiana (print) 20230191053 | Canadiana (ebook) 2023019124X | ISBN 9781927886724 (softcover) | ISBN 9781927886731 (ebook)
Subjects: LCSH: Indigenous peoples—Manitoba—Winnipeg—Economic conditions—20th century. | LCSH: Indigenous peoples—Manitoba—Winnipeg—Social conditions—20th century. | LCSH: Indigenous peoples—Housing—Manitoba—Winnipeg—History—20th century. | LCSH: Economic development—Manitoba—Winnipeg—History—20th century. | LCSH: Social planning—Manitoba—Winnipeg—History—20th century. | LCSH: Indigenous peoples—Manitoba—Winnipeg—Politics and government—History—20th century. | CSH: Indigenous activists—Manitoba—Winnipeg—History—20th century.
Classification: LCC E78.M25 I53 2023 | DDC 330.90089/970712743—dc23

Indigenous Resistance and Development in Winnipeg: 1960–2000

Shauna MacKinnon and Kathy Mallett, Editors

Winnipeg | ARP Books

Table of Contents

Forward

Resistance and Development:

Indigenous Organizations in Winnipeg

Nicole Lamy

My name is Nicole Lamy. I am from the city of Winnipeg, which is located on Treaty 1 territory and on the homeland of the Métis. I am the director of community engagement for Merchants Corner Inc., a housing development which is situated on Selkirk Avenue in the North End neighbourhood where I grew up. I am of Métis, Anishinaabe Saulteaux descent. I am a member of O-Chi-Chak-Ko-Sipi First Nation, also known as Crane River. My paternal granny was a First Nation woman from O-Chi-Chak-Ko-Sipi Nation. My maternal grandmother (Mamere) is a Michif woman from St. Laurent, a small community located on the homeland of the Métis Nation in Manitoba. I grew up in a large Indigenous family, fortunate to have been surrounded by the voices of powerful women. In 2014, I graduated with a Bachelor of Arts degree with a major in Urban and Inner-City Studies. The Department of Urban and Inner-City Studies is located on Selkirk Avenue at Merchants Corner where I currently work. Since graduating, I have worked in the non-profit sector in the field of community development. My experience growing up and studying in the North End has shaped my identity, my career goals, and the way I try to make a difference in the world for Indigenous people.

I am honoured to have had the opportunity to listen to interviews with Indigenous people who were leaders in the development of Indigenous-led organizations in Winnipeg. The Preserving the History of Aboriginal Institutional Development in Winnipeg project, which forms the basis of this book, was in Indigenous-led research project that sought to preserve the history of Indigenous organizing and development in Winnipeg, in part by providing a space for these leaders to share their stories in the form of a series of interviews. These video-recorded interviews capture the experiences of people familiar to me and others I had not heard before. A few of the people interviewed have since passed on, so it was particularly powerful to hear their voices.

When I first began to listen to the interviews, I felt very self-conscious about my lack of knowledge of Indigenous activism in Winnipeg. I did not know about the challenges these leaders had faced and the long and difficult road that led to the development of many of the institutions we often take for granted today. We didn't learn about this part of our history in school, so growing up I was not aware of this local Indigenous activism. I didn't realize that people were protesting at the legislature, challenging the child welfare and justice systems. And I did not know that Indigenous people in my community were protesting in solidarity with their Mohawk relatives in Oka and with Indigenous peoples across Turtle Island. As I listened to the interviews, I felt sad about my lack of knowledge of the Indigenous activism in my community, but I also felt very inspired. I felt a comfort in listening to these voices I related with. Like them, I find there are certain places in Winnipeg where I would prefer to be because I know that other Indigenous people gather in these spaces. I also realize that there were fewer of these spaces in the past than there are today, and I am thankful to those responsible for creating them. They offer Indigenous people like me a greater sense of belonging and pride.

One theme that came up in almost every interview I listened to was that many of those interviewed grew up to internalize a feeling of shame. I very much related with this feeling. I too have not always felt proud to be Indigenous. Learning about the history of strong Indigenous women gave me more strength to resist the racism I learned to internalize. I listened to stories from women like Louise Chippeway, who explained, "I would tell myself—be proud of who you are, to be proud to be Aboriginal. Go out and get involved." This theme of overcoming shame through strength and resistance was present throughout the interviews as these Indigenous leaders shared stories about how they fought to build a better community for future generations. I was inspired by their stories. They gave me a new perspective on my responsibility as an Indigenous woman, who, as described by Vern Morrissette, "stands on the shoulders of those who came before us." Through their stories, I learned of the love and perseverance that led to the development of Indigenous organizations that have existed throughout my lifetime. These are the places that I've known to be safe for Indigenous people to go get support or services, or to simply be with other Indigenous people.

One of the places I learned more about, where I spent time at as a youth and young adult, was the Indian and Métis Friendship Centre (IMFC). The history of the Indigenization of the IMFC was particularly inspiring to me. I fondly recall many different community gatherings at the centre at the corner of Robinson Street and Dufferin Avenue. There I attended many pancake breakfasts, holiday events, and some of my favourite socials. I recall volunteering at the IMFC for the Christmas holiday celebration, where I helped in the kitchen to feed over 500 people. I recall proudly attending my cousin's first CD-release party at the IMFC, featuring his band's traditional Métis fiddle music. But I hadn't given much thought to how the IMFC came to be. I did not know that the IMFC was initially located on Donald Street and had relocated to various other locations to accommodate its growth. I was surprised to learn that the IMFC initially began with a non-Indigenous board, and I was proud to learn about the Indigenous women and men who were instrumental to its transformation.

Louise Chippeway's interview stood out to me because she spoke of her work in the early days with the IMFC. She shared stories about the Purple Pit, where local artists would come and play music. It sounded like a hot spot for gathering around Indigenous music and celebrations. She described the IMFC as the place where everything was happening and where Indigenous activism was centered. This was the place that taught her to be proud to be an Indigenous person. The IMFC was a place where Indigenous people moving to the city could access support and resources such as housing. People were able to get involved in all aspects of the centre, which provided a safe place for social activism and support. The experience Chippeway described of feeling safe and respected at the IMFC was similar to mine, and it was nice to hear her perspective on the centre's history and the work that she was involved in, surveying the community about their housing needs. Chippeway's passion for the community really came through in her interview, and this left me feeling inspired to continue trying to make a difference for Indigenous people and reaffirmed for me the importance of community conversations.

Learning about Ma Mawi Wi Chi Itata Centre's history was also very powerful for me. I've had friends who attended programs at Ma Mawi Wi Chi Itata Centre. They were drawn to it because of its Indigenous focus and the sense of belonging they felt there. It was important for me to learn that, throughout its history, there were challenges along the way and people didn't always agree on everything. Hearing Kathy Mallett talk about her experiences as a founder and board member of Ma Mawi Wi Chi Itata Centre was inspiring to me. She spoke of challenges along the way. Learning from Kathy Mallett and Josie Hill about the challenges the board members faced and the philosophical differences that came up and how they overcame them was an important teaching for me. Despite the challenges, the board was able to move forward in a respectful and kind way, always keeping the focus on, "How best can we do this for the community?" I realize that many organizations experience growing pains, and it is important that we work through our differences and put the community first. Ma Mawi Wi Chi Itata Centre has persevered through many challenges and has persevered to serve Indigenous children and families. I enjoyed hearing Josie Hill share her experience returning to Ma Mawi Wi Chi Itata Centre as the executive director at a time when circumstances had led it to stray from its community roots, but a strong sense of community ensured its return. This made me reflect on the importance of Indigenous organizations remaining grounded in community.

Although it wasn't always overtly stated in the interviews, it became clear to me that strong Indigenous women leadership was central to the success of Indigenous led organizations in Winnipeg, as well as the philosophy that continues to guide them I had not heard of the "Indian Rights Women Group" until listening to Kathy Mallett speak about it, and I did not know about the women involved. As an Indigenous woman who grew up surrounded by aunties, there is something that makes these organizations even more special to me when I learn about the role of Indigenous women. I really felt connected with the approach that Mallett described. She emphasized the importance of "listening... cause all these women had stories, you know? And so just learning stories and, and really forming relationships with them was the greatest thing." Mallett said that they would use the women's stories to strategize and figure out how to best tackle issues. This also reminded me of how working in the inner city often involves finding creative solutions to complex problems. Lucille Bruce talked about the importance of taking time when making big decisions that will affect people's lives. We often feel pressure to move and respond quickly, and I appreciated hearing how Bruce took time to think things through before taking on important community roles. She also reminded me that sometimes our roles in community change and evolve as we grow as leaders. In each of the interviews I listened to, it was clear that everyone was focused on working in a relational way to create places for people to gather and to challenge oppressive systems to ensure that future generations would not experience the racism that they knew all too well. They were driven by their desire for future generations to be proud and strong Indigenous people.

Stan McKay shared one of my favourite stories. He talked about living in the North when training to be a United Church minister. He said that while he spent a lot of time listening and learning from non-Indigenous pastors, his most important learning came from an Indigenous elder who took him out to a pine tree and shared teachings with him. There he learned of the importance of being connected to the land. Vern Morrissette spoke about connection to the land as well. This resonated with me because an important part of my learning has also come through teachings on the land. Although I was raised in the city, we often visited our family "in the bush" around St. Laurent. My auntie would pick me up and bring me to her home where she would play fiddle music and teach me how to jig. Like Vern, who described himself as an "urban Indian" who spent time on the land with his extended family, I would return home to the city after my visits. But my connection to the land was strong, and I felt proud of where I came from. Like Vern, this gave me strength to deal with the racism that I felt in the city. Also like Vern, being from a big Indigenous family made me stronger, and I felt "rich in other ways." As a "North Ender," the feeling of being rich in other ways is something that seems to be "in the air" in the North End, and it's part of the reason why Indigenous people feel at home here.

As I reflect on what I have learned from listening to the interviews that form the basis of this book, the words of Stan McKay—"we will respect each other; respect the earth and we will work together"—remind me that we are stronger when we work together and learn from one another. Working in the inner city and with Indigenous people has taught me that there is no quick fix when dealing with issues. It is important to listen to community voices and seek creative solutions.

Learning about the history of the community I live and work in gives me a deeper appreciation and respect for those who came before me. Feeling a connection with and learning from these leaders helps me in my work when I am feeling discouraged. These leaders persevered despite the challenges they faced. They did not give up the fight. They were determined that Indigenous people would make decisions for Indigenous people. The women leaders were particularly strong and inspiring, tirelessly and bravely supporting each other as they stood up against colonial institutions and systemic injustices, often without pay and while caring for their families. Because of their commitment and determination, Indigenous organizations and education programs are thriving. Opportunities for Indigenous people in the community have significantly grown. I feel that there has been a noticeable shift; we are taking back our spaces and controlling the way we learn, support each other, and teach and inspire the future generations. Systems are beginning to be transformed to better serve our community. This shift did not simply happen on its own. It is the legacy of the many Indigenous women and men who demanded better. It is now the responsibility of my generation to carry on this work.

As an Indigenous leader in community development in the inner city, things can be very challenging as we continue to fight against systemic barriers. The interviews reminded me of why I do this work, and they reminded me of the importance of ensuring that Indigenous values and traditions are prominent in the work. They reminded me of the importance of creating space for our Indigenous cultures and traditions to flourish in the community, and I have now instituted the practice of Indigenous teachings for community members at Merchants Corner. Even though we are of different generations, our stories about where we grew up, our work and education experiences, the challenges that we have experienced, and the journeys to learn more about our Indigenous cultures are similar.

There is a beautiful Indigenous community in Winnipeg that is full of love, life, and support. I have been reminded by those who came before me that community work is slow, challenging, and at times, heavy. I need to be patient. I need to take time to remember to smudge and pray. I need to take time to celebrate our community, our knowledge keepers, our elders, and our youth. There remains much to learn and unlearn. Building on the safe spaces created by past leaders and working collectively will make us stronger.

As described through the stories in this book, the journey of Indigenous resistance and development in Winnipeg has been long and difficult, but gratifying. And it continues. Indigenous people in Winnipeg continue to fight for better housing, education, emancipation from oppressive colonial systems, and improved Indigenous-led resources and supports. But the path has been cleared and I'm thankful for the ones that have helped pave it for my generation. They remind us to persevere when things get difficult. They remind us of what is possible. They give me strength.

Introduction

Shauna MacKinnon and Kathy Mallett

In the 1950s, growing numbers of Indigenous people began moving to Winnipeg from rural and northern Manitoba. Their reasons were diverse, but many people moved to the city seeking opportunities not available in their home communities. Housing on reserves was poor, and access to education was limited. Post-secondary education was non-existent.

The city, they thought, offered a better life. Many came with trepidation but also with hopes and dreams for themselves and their families. They quickly learned that Winnipeg was not a welcoming place. They were all too often viewed as dirty, dangerous, and indigent. Many landlords would not rent to them. They were lucky to get hired, and when they did, the work was hard, poorly paid, and often short term. Those living with the trauma of residential school experiences remained suspicious of the school system and its motives. They discovered that their children's teachers did not share their cultures and experiences, and the curriculum either ignored them entirely or presented them as inferior. Their children could not relate with their teachers, and racism in schools was rampant. Parents struggling in poverty wanted a better future for their children, only to discover that a child welfare system that was supposed to help them saw fit to blame them and punish them by taking their children. Far too many families became entangled in that system and were deeply damaged by it. Those who came to the city to enjoy the promise of personal freedom—part of the allure of a big city—found themselves marginalized and victimized. Some came speaking little English, only to be told their languages were dead, best forgotten. Despite systemic racism and unrelenting obstacles, Indigenous people in Winnipeg demanded more for themselves, their families, and their communities. They began to organize.

This book offers a glimpse into the history of Indigenous resistance and resilience during the latter part of the twentieth century. Through the voices of those who were involved, it tells little known stories behind the organizing and development of Indigenous institutions in Winnipeg that many are familiar with, if only in name. This book describes the Indigenizing of the Indian and Métis Friendship Centre (IMFC), the seedbed of Indigenous activism in Winnipeg beginning in the 1950s. The IMFC provided a safe place for Indigenous people to visit over tea and bannock, share stories in their Native languages, and talk about the problems they faced. There they developed allies in the Winnipeg community and learned from examples of Indigenous resistance elsewhere. Those involved in the IMFC envisioned and later created their own institutions to realize their visions. The IMFC was an incubator for a number of initiatives, including the role it played in bringing twenty-one Native organizations in Winnipeg together to develop a comprehensive social and economic development proposal which later inspired the development of the Aboriginal Centre.

Activists share their stories of resistance to a racist child welfare system and how that led to the creation of the Ma Mawi Wi Chi Itata child and family services agency. Others share their memories of a groundswell of activism that led to the creation of two schools for Indigenous children: Children of the Earth and Niji Mahkwa schools. Community economic development approaches flourished during this period as evidenced by the stories describing the history of Neechi Foods Co-op, Payuk Housing, and Kinew Housing. Readers will be inspired by the determination of the 2SLGBQT community who mobilized to create Nichiwakan Native Gay Society.

Some of these organizations live on today, others have been transformed, and some have fallen by the wayside. In all cases, they made a difference. But these organizations and the people who created and nurtured them have largely been ignored by history. In 2011, a group of Indigenous activists and university scholars led by Kathy Mallett and John Loxley aimed to change this. With the support of the Manitoba Research Alliance, a community-university research collaboration administered by the Canadian Centre for Policy Alternatives (Manitoba Office), the Preserving the History of Aboriginal Institutional Development in Winnipeg project hired community researchers Darrell Chippeway and Larry Morrissette. They gathered historical documents and interviewed Indigenous people actively engaged in Indigenous resistance and development during the latter part of the twentieth century.

The video interviews and historical documents are now preserved at the University of Manitoba Archives. This book synthesizes the oral histories and documents gathered through the Preserving the History of Aboriginal Institutional Development in Winnipeg project. It honours the work of those interviewed and ensures that their stories are accessible to students and others interested in this little-known history of Winnipeg.

Limitations and Omissions

This book includes nine chapters, but we are keenly aware that it might have included many more. We chose topics that align with some of the key themes that emerged from the interviews conducted by Darrell Chippeway and Larry Morrissette. Our book is by no means complete. There are many more stories to tell. New Indigenous organizations have emerged in the early part of the twenty-first century. Old problems persist and have taken new forms; new challenges arise and summon a new generation of activists into the struggle. We are acutely aware of the need to do more work on the contributions of Indigenous women; on the systemic racism and violence that characterizes the way the law, the courts, and the police treat Indigenous people; on the careers of Indigenous politicians; and on the roles that elders have played in sustaining community and culture.

Throughout the interviews, we heard about the important roles of Indigenous women. While women feature prominently in each of the chapters in this book, there is far more that could be said. Vern Morrissette noted in his 2013 interview with his brother Larry, and Darrell Chippeway that women were—are—"the true leaders." Doris Young graciously contributed a chapter on her experience creating and sustaining a province-wide organization for Indigenous women. But there are many more stories. The behind-the-scenes work Indigenous women have carried has often been hidden from history. A former Grand Chief of the Assembly of Manitoba Chiefs (AMC) acknowledged this on the AMC website when he described the significant role of women in the development of "Wahbung: Our Tomorrows," a paper outlining a vision for Indigenous peoples in Manitoba that continues to provide guidance to Indigenous organizations today.

While this book highlights a number of organizations that Indigenous women have played a role in establishing, particularly Ma Mawi Wi Chi Itata Centre, there are many more organizations that await their own recorded histories. These include the These include Ikwe Widdjiitiwin crisis shelter, Ndiniwe safe house for at-risk youth, Oyate Tipi furniture bank, and Wahbung Abinoonjiaag, which offers programs for youth and women experiencing violence. Additionally, women led the development of Ka Ni Kanichihk, which offers Indigenous led prevention and intervention progams, Mother of Red Nations Women's Council of Manitoba (MORN), which supports and advocates for Indigenous women and children, Blue Thunderbird Family Care, and Granny's House, which provide supports for Indigenous families Women currently leading these organizations were mentored by those who came before them, and they are now mentoring the next generation of women leaders. They will have their own stories to tell.

Indigenous activists have challenged systemic racism in other areas not fully captured in this book. There is much more to be said about Indigenous resistance to systemic racism in policing and the criminal justice system and healthcare during the 1980s and 1990s. For example, the Aboriginal Justice Inquiry (AJI) was a critical event in Manitoba's history that culminated from Indigenous activism and outrage over systemic racism, injustice, and state violence toward Indigenous peoples. In 1988, two events galvanized Indigenous people in Manitoba: the shooting death of Indigenous leader J.J. Harper and the trial of two men for the murder of Helen Betty Osborne, a young Indigenous woman in the town of The Pas. These shocking events led to the appointment of a provincial inquiry into the justice system in Manitoba. Murray Sinclair, an Indigenous provincial court judge, was appointed as a co-commissioner of the AJI. Along with his co-commissioner Justice Alvin Hamilton, Sinclair conducted a high-profile investigation into these cases and the broader system. The commission highlighted the violence and systemic racism of the justice system and offered a vision of a different model that recognized Indigenous rights to self-government. That vision has not been realized, but important initiatives, particularly in the field of child welfare, flow from the commission's final report. Although the recommendations put forward by the Report of the Aboriginal Justice Inquiry were not fully implemented, the commission set in motion several important systemic changes. It is an important historical record of systemic injustices that remains relevant today. The ongoing work that Indigenous people have taken both inside the justice system and in identifying its horrifying failures await their historians.

Indigenous people have established their own political organizations. In the 1960s, they played a key role in defeating a federal government attempt to end its historic responsibilities to Indigenous people. From the local to the national level, Manitoba has produced generations of effective political leaders. In increasing numbers, Indigenous people have also engaged in politics at the municipal, provincial, and federal levels, holding elected and appointed office. While some of their stories have been documented, others have yet to be told. The important role that elders and Indigenous knowledge keepers played in past organizing is also missing from this book. Many of those interviewed spoke of the inspiration that came from their elders and many are now themselves respected elders in their communities, inspiring a new generation of community leaders. Despite its limitations, we hope that this book offers a glimpse into Indigenous resistance and development in Winnipeg during the latter part of the twentieth century.

This book was initially developed with a specific audience in mind—second-year university students. However, we believe it will appeal to many others. This book is also a gesture of honouring past contributions by Indigenous people committed to challenging colonialism, reclaiming sovereignty, and making the world a better place for generations to follow.

Acknowledgements

To say that compiling this collection has been a challenge is an understatement. The loss of our dear friend and collaborator John Loxley was a major setback. It took us several months to get back on track after his death in July 2020. Although he passed before we were able to complete this collection, he was with us in spirit throughout the project. He was deeply committed to Kathy Mallett's vision of creating a forum for sharing the oral histories and written records of the Indigenous people involved in resistance and development in the latter part of the twentieth century.

Larry Morrissette left us to join the spirit world in 2016. Larry was instrumental to the Preserving the History Aboriginal Institutional Development in Winnipeg project. His passing was a reminder of why it is so important to capture these stories and honour the contributions of those who are still with us, while they are still with us.

We did most of this work during the Covid-19 pandemic, which seriously limited our access to the documents now held at the University of Manitoba. The pandemic also made it impossible for us to have the kinds of in-person conversations that we would typically have had. Thankfully we were able to access most of the interviews conducted by Darrell Chippeway and Larry Morrissette through the Preserving Aboriginal History Project. Kathy Mallett had a box or two of documents preserved at her home which also helped. Authors also benefited greatly from zoom chats, telephone conversations, and email exchanges with Flora Zaharia, Bill Sanderson, Vern Morrissette, Joe Keeper, Linda Keeper, Linda Clarkson, Marion Meadmore and Josie Hill. We are immensely grateful for their time, and we owe a depth of gratitude to all who participated in the interviews with Larry and Darrell. This book would not exist without you.

Full interviews with each of these remarkable people are available at the University of Manitoba Archives. Thematic audio productions are available through the University of Winnipeg Department of Urban and Inner-City Studies and the Manitoba Research Alliance through the Canadian Centre for Policy Alternatives-Manitoba.

Dedication

This book is dedicated to Larry Morrissette and John Loxley. Both Larry and John were deeply committed to the preservation of the history of Indigenous activism in Winnipeg. Remembering their commitment inspired us to complete this book at times when it became difficult. They are deeply missed and always remembered.

All proceeds from the sale of this book will go to the Larry Morrissette Scholarship to support Indigenous students studying in the Department of Urban and Inner and Inner-City Studies at the University of Winnipeg.

We also dedicate this book to the men and women who were interviewed for the Preserving Aboriginal History in Winnipeg Project. They include: Marileen Bartlett; Jim Bear; Barbara Bruce; Lucille Bruce;

Ann Callahan; Louise Champagne; Ivy Chaske; Louise Chippeway; Glenn Cochrane; Mary Courchene; Elaine Cowan; Dennis Daniels; Janet Fontaine; Lena Friesen; Mary Guilbault; Wayne Helgason; Dan Highway; Josie Hill; Damon Johnston; Cyril Keeper; Joe Keeper; Linda Keeper; Jackie Lavallee; Stan McKay; Kathy Mallett; Albert McLeod; Norman Mead; Marion Meadmore; Vern Morrissette; George Munroe; Ruth Murdock; Barbara Nepinak; Clarence Nepinak; Eric Robinson; Francis Roesely; Bill Shead; Murray Sinclair; Leslie Spillett; Doris Young; Flora Zaharia

Chapter 1

Preserving the History of Aboriginal Institutional Development in Winnipeg:

Research Driven by the Community[1]

John Loxley and Kathy Mallett

In 2008, an Indigenous-led consortium of activists and academics initiated a research project called Preserving the History of Aboriginal Institutional Development in Winnipeg. In this chapter, the authors who also led the project, more commonly known as the Indigenous Archives Project, describe how it led to the preservation of records in the University of Manitoba, Indigenous Peoples Collection. The project, completed in 2013, is an example of how Indigenous activists, community researchers, and academics can work collaboratively to ensure the preservation of urban Indigenous history.

The project was financed through three Government of Canada Tri-Council Social Science and Humanities Research Council (SSHRC) programs. Primary support was provided through the

1 This chapter is a revision of John Loxley and Evelyn Peters' "Preserving the History of Indigenous Institutional Development in Winnipeg: Research Driven by the Community," in *Practising Community-Based Participatory Research: Stories of Engagement, Empowerment and Mobilization*, ed. Shauna MacKinnon (Vancouver: UBC-Purich Press, 2018, 193-212.)

Transforming Inner-City and Aboriginal Communities Project (2007–2012) and Partnering for Change: Community-Based Solutions for Aboriginal and Inner-City Poverty (2012–2020). These SSHRC-funded projects were led by University of Manitoba economist and principal investigator Dr. John Loxley through the Manitoba Research Alliance (MRA). Dr. Evelyn Peters provided financial support through a Tri-Council Grant awarded to her as the Canada Research Chair (CRC) in Inner-City Issues, Community Learning, and Engagement, situated at the University of Winnipeg.

The purpose of the project was three-fold: first, to collect historical documents capturing Indigenous activism in Winnipeg (we believed these documents were disbursed across the city at the organizations themselves, as well as in the homes of the activists involved in the development of the organizations); second, to record the oral histories of Indigenous activists involved in the development of Indigenous organizations in Winnipeg; and third, to find a permanent home for these records so that they would be accessible to scholars, students, and the broader public.

Preservation of and access to these materials were much needed and long overdue. Early Indigenous institutions have not had a history of archiving their records for two reasons: first, no one thought about it; and second, there wasn't time.[2] The Indigenous Archives Project captures a portion of the history of urban Indigenous activism that the people involved in the activism were too busy to document at the time. As Indigenous activist Kathy Mallett describes (and as past director of the Native Women's Transition Centre Lucille Bruce echoes), "We didn't document things very well, we were so busy doing the work ... A lot of the work we were doing was organic and we didn't have a lot of funds to do it. We were responding to the issues of the day."[3] At

2 Darrell Chippeway, *A Report on Preserving the History of Aboriginal Institutional Development in Winnipeg Project* (Winnipeg: Manitoba Research Alliance, 2013)

3 Kathy Mallett in Carol Sanders, "Putting Together a Piece of History," *Winnipeg Free* Press, March 4, 2013, A6.

the same time, the women activists—and there were many who played pivotal roles in institutional development in Winnipeg—were also "the ones raising the children and looking after the seniors. You've got to be responsible for your community."[4] In that situation, the historical record takes a distinctly secondary place to the activism and to the challenges of daily life, and in many cases the events go unrecorded or the paper trail disappears "in a dumpster."[5] This project helps to preserve that record to some extent.

Although collecting the documented history was more challenging than anticipated, it was possible to obtain important records. The historical records of the Indian and Métis Friendship Centre (IMFC) are particularly important to the continuity of the organization, given the centrality of the IMFC in urban Indigenous historical experience. Although not all records survived, Lena Friesen, who was the executive director of the IMFC in the early 1980s, provided a number of documents. Equally important are the voluminous paper files of the Aboriginal Council of Winnipeg and of several other Aboriginal organizations housed in the Aboriginal Centre which might not have survived were it not for this project.[6] Larry Morrissette donated a history he had written of the Ma Mawi Wi Chi Itata Centre for a conference held in Albuquerque, New Mexico in 1988, and Louise Chippeway donated an Aboriginal Housing study she wrote in 1971. Ivy Chaske submitted pictures from various urban Aboriginal conferences and gatherings from the 1980s.[7]

As we endeavoured to collect historical documents, the recording of oral histories became an increasingly important part of this project. By 2012, a project which started with one researcher and one student

4 Ibid. ibid.

5 ibid.

6 Jesse Boiteau, "Co-curation and Participatory Archives," presentation to symposium, *I Have Never Forgotten His Words… Talking about Indigenous Archives*, at the Institute for the Humanities, University of Manitoba, October 5, 2013.

7 Chippeway, *A Report*, 3.

ended with a team of fifteen participants with varying degrees of involvement, ten of whom were Indigenous and seven of whom were students. The project is an excellent, if rare, example of co-curation and participatory archiving.[8]

Project Overview

The Indigenous Archives Project was undertaken by Indigenous activists and ally academics. They were concerned that the history of Indigenous activism in the latter part of the twentieth century faced the prospect of not being recorded at all. The Indigenous Archives Project became a priority project for MRA researchers who worked with members of the Indigenous community to identify initiatives whose documents were not archived, and then the researchers put together whatever written records existed to ensure their preservation and accessibility at an archival institution or library. Through the MRA, researchers hired a member of the Indigenous community familiar with Winnipeg's Indigenous history to work with them, along with a student archivist. They sought out written documents for preservation. They video-recorded interviews of key actors where written records either did not exist or were deficient. These recordings would later be included in the Indigenous Peoples Collection at the University of Manitoba. More than 100 hours of video-recorded interviews with Indigenous activists involved throughout the 1960s and 1990s are now preserved at the university. These materials are being used to generate educational materials for at least one university course. Their preservation will ensure that this history of Indigenous development in Winnipeg is accessible and told through the voices of those involved.

Project Team

The Indigenous Archives Project was initiated by Kathy Mallett. Kathy had been involved in several Indigenous activist initiatives in

8 Boiteau, "Co-curation and Participatory Archives."

the 1980s and 1990s and was concerned about the fact that the story about the legacy of activist efforts had not been documented. The activists involved in this work were getting on in years and it was important to her that their stories be told so that a new generation of Indigenous activists would know of the work that preceded them. Mallett, a member of the Manitoba Research Alliance, raised the idea with MRA principal investigator John Loxley. The MRA is a unique research partnership between the university and the community. It is among the few academic-community research consortia administered through a non-profit organization—in this case the Canadian Centre for Policy Alternatives—that has been awarded institutional eligibility and funding from SSHRC.

John Loxley had a strong research record and a well-established relationship with Indigenous communities in Manitoba. In the 1990s, he was called on to contribute to the Royal Commission on Aboriginal Peoples. His work included research on Aboriginal Economic Development in Winnipeg, a modified form of which was published in 2000.[9] Later he sought to document, analyze, and preserve alternative Indigenous approaches to economic development that were evident in the city of Winnipeg.[10] Looking at the institutional developments around these approaches and seeking to preserve their records seemed to be a logical and worthwhile extension of Loxley's earlier work. Evelyn Peters was invited to participate in the project given her role as CRC at the University of Winnipeg, her collaboration with the MRA, and her long history of recording Aboriginal institutional development across Canada, especially urban institutional

9 Loxley et al., *Aboriginal People in the Winnipeg Economy*, Royal Commission on Aboriginal Peoples, Ottawa, Volume 5, 1996 (Appendix B), http://www.collectionscanada.gc.ca/webarchives/20071124124835/; https://publications.gc.ca/collections/collection_2017/bcp-pco/Z1-1991-1-41-161-eng.pdf.; Jim Silver, *Solutions That Work: Fighting Poverty in Winnipeg* (Winnipeg: Canadian Centre for Policy Alternatives-Manitoba; Winnipeg: Fernwood Publishing, 2000)

10 See John Loxley, *Aboriginal, Northern, and Community Economic Development: Papers and Retrospectives* (Winnipeg: ARP Books, 2010).

arrangements. Some of her work already encompassed important institutions in Winnipeg such as the Indian and Métis Friendship Centre and Indigenous women's initiatives.[11]

The Evolution of the Project

Before the project was fully formed, the preliminary step Loxley, Mallett, and Peters took was to hire Jesse Boiteau—a graduate student in the University of Manitoba's Archival Studies Program—to conduct a scan of relevant materials that already existed in various libraries and archives in the city. He examined books, academic and popular articles, newspapers and reports, as well as websites referring to Indigenous organizations, to ascertain the institutional landscape. Then he tried to find materials for these institutions in archives and libraries to assess the level of "archival integration."[12] Over forty Indigenous organizations were identified, almost all of which were still operating in 2008. Boiteau provided a brief description of the function of each organization, together with addresses and contact numbers. Where such information was not forthcoming, he noted the text or texts which referenced its existence. Finding sources for these organizations in the two main archives—the Archives of Manitoba and the University of Manitoba Archives—was, however, very rare.[13] Researchers approached the City of Winnipeg Archives for assistance in locating documentation but did not receive a response. This research formed the foundation for the second phase of the project, in which researchers sought out records and interviewed those involved. In the meantime, however, the organization and methodology of the research had begun to transform.

11 Evelyn Peters, "'The Two Major Living Realities': Urban Services Needs of First Nations Women in Canadian Cities,'" in *Gendering the City: Women, Boundaries and Visions of Urban Life*, ed. Kristine B. Miranne and Alma H. Young (Lanham MD: Rowman and Littlefield, 2000)

12 Graham Stinnett, *Urban Aboriginal Organizations*, Report on Research Progress, November 24, 2008, 1.

13 Peters, "'The Two Major Living Realities,'" 17.

The second phase of the project saw it evolve from being a university-based archival research project undertaken by non-Indigenous researchers to becoming a joint community-university-based project with a majority of Indigenous input. A Research Advisory Committee was formed consisting of Loxley and Peters, and long-time Indigenous activists Kathy Mallett, Louise Chippeway, and Larry Morrissette. Each had a long history of involvement in the development of Indigenous institutions in Winnipeg. Kathy Mallett also had experience as an archivist working in the Archives of Manitoba. Louise Chippeway was the managing editor of a report commemorating the twenty-five years of service of the Indian and Métis Friendship Centre of Winnipeg, honouring "the people who worked hard to make it a success." And Larry Morrissette had been heavily involved in the repatriation of Indian artifacts from institutions in Winnipeg to their home communities in Manitoba First Nations.[14] The group brought many years of practical and organizational experience to the project, giving it a clear, Indigenous-led direction. The committee met at least monthly between 2009 and 2012 and oversaw critical decisions.

The advisory committee hired Darrell Chippeway, a student and a First Nation journalist who had worked with the Canadian Broadcasting Corporation (CBC). Darrell assumed the key role in advancing the project on the ground. While the collection of paper archives slowly progressed, a decision was made to shift the focus to digital interviews of Indigenous activists. Darrell argued—and the committee agreed—that video-recorded oral histories would provide a richer account of activist experiences and would be accessible to a broader audience. The committee then hired Crystal Greene, another young Indigenous student who had worked with the CBC, to do the video recording. Later in the project, Crystal was joined by Darryl Nepinak, an experienced Aboriginal videographer and filmmaker.

14 Indian and Métis Friendship Centre, *History of the Winnipeg Indian and Métis Friendship Centre, 1958–1983: 25 Years of Service and Development in the Winnipeg Community* (Winnipeg: IMFC, 1983), 2.

The advisory committee met several times to determine who to interview. The focus was to be mainly on Indigenous elders and other Indigenous activists who had worked extensively, though not exclusively, in Winnipeg. The committee and staff started by identifying key activists for interview. Additional people were selected through snowball sampling, a recruitment technique that involves interview participants identifying other potential participants who meet the study criteria. Snowball sampling was particularly effective for this project given the close relationships among Indigenous activists in Winnipeg. A total of fifty-one possible interviewees were identified, twenty-seven being female and twenty-four being male. A secondary list of sixteen individuals was also developed, to be drawn upon if time and money permitted. The committee agreed to an interview process and developed an interview guide. The process was vetted and approved through the University of Manitoba Joint-Faculty Research Ethics Board (REB).

Research Ethics

Each person to be interviewed was approached for a pre-interview. Notes were written up and submitted to members of the advisory committee for comment. This process helped to formulate guidance and structure for the video recording without being overly prescriptive. The committee agreed that they wanted to encourage a spontaneous and relaxed environment to allow participants to share their stories in their own way.

It became apparent early in the interview process that the technical expertise of the young interviewers would be complemented by the presence of one of the Indigenous members of the Research Advisory Committee with more knowledge of the historical, institutional, and political landscape of Winnipeg. Longtime Indigenous activist and committee member Larry Morrissette agreed to become part of that process. He prepared an information letter which was circulated to prospective interview participants. He emphasized the importance of the project in preserving for future generations important aspects of Indigenous history in Winnipeg. The letter invited recipients to participate in videorecording interviews to be conducted at the Manitoba Indigenous Cultural Education Centre. He also encouraged them to bring with them any written records they might have to be deposited for safekeeping with other archival information gathered through the project. A list of suggested questions was prepared (appendix 2) and provided in advance to interviewees. Invited participants consented to participate by signing the REB-approved informed consent form that described the parameters of the project (appendix 1).

The Interviews

The advisory committee developed a series of interview questions over several meetings. They were designed to elicit from those interviewed stories about how they came to reside in Winnipeg, what relationships they maintained with their home community, their education trajectory, and their recollection of institutional supports available to them. Interview participants were asked about the roles they and other Indigenous people played in building institutions in the city and how these institutions performed. Participants were asked to comment on their perceptions of existing Indigenous organizations, including their strengths and weaknesses. They were asked specifically to comment on the role of women and the principles underlying their activities. They were also asked to describe any various approaches to community economic development that they might have been involved with or observed and, in particular, the contrast between collectivist and private enterprise approaches.[15] Finally, participants were asked to compare the current context in Winnipeg with what they experienced in the past, their perceptions of their children and grandchildren's experiences, and what might be done by contemporary Indigenous youth to improve Indigenous-led institutions. Since draft questions

15 See Chapter 7 in Loxley et al., *Aboriginal, Northern, and Community Economic Development.*

were prepared for each interview, there were always opportunities to adjust the standard questions to engage the interviewees more fully and to draw out their specific experiences.

Other chapters in this collection draw on the forty-plus interviews collected in the videos to describe in greater detail the development of various institutions and initiatives. The interviews include a blend of individual life stories describing personal struggles and achievements, as well as reflections on the work involved in developing Indigenous institutions. Interviewees also shared their personal perspectives about the effects of colonialism and racism to which Indigenous people are routinely subjected. As Chippeway describes, colonialism, racism, the activism that led to the development of Indigenous institutions, and the growth of individuals involved, were interrelated and connected.[16]

Choosing a Location to House the Archive

From the outset of the project, an important issue was the choice of where to safely store and archive materials collected by the project. Members of the advisory committee met with the provincial archivist who was very supportive of the project, but who concluded that the rules and restrictions at the Archives of Manitoba were ill-suited to it. The problems were two-fold: one, the archives would only accept original records and not copies; and two, once materials had been donated under a Certificate of Gift between the donor organization and the archives, the material would become the property of the archives. It was felt that both provisions were unduly restrictive, especially the second, as members of the advisory committee did not want to rule out the possibility that an Aboriginal archive might take possession of the material at some point in the future. Discussions were also held at the new Canadian Museum of Human Rights, and again, the archivist there was very supportive but felt that due to the museum being in its

16 Chippeway, *A Report*

infancy, it may not have the capacity needed to immediately handle the materials being generated by the project.

The advisory committee then organized formal interviews with the archivists from the University of Winnipeg (U of W) and the University of Manitoba (U of M). To that point in time, the committee had been leaning in the direction of the University of Winnipeg Archives as the repository for a number of reasons. First, its location in downtown Winnipeg is very central and therefore more accessible. Secondly, U of W had made Indigenous issues a major priority and had built some important programs aimed at the Indigenous community at both the graduate level (for example a Master of Arts in Indigenous Governance and a Master of Development Practice in Indigenous Development) and undergraduate level (a Bachelor of Arts in Indigenous Studies and a Bachelor of Arts in Urban and Inner-City Studies). And thirdly, an increasingly large share of the funding for the Indigenous Archives Project was being provided by Evelyn Peters' CRC funding held at the university. In the end, the committee chose the U of M because it was better equipped in terms of space, technology, and staffing. At that time, the U of M protocols for Indigenous materials were more advanced than those at U of W, and had an emphasis on stewardship as opposed to ownership of materials. Further, the close association of the university archive with the Archival Studies program and its students seemed to offer a more integrated and comprehensive package of assistance to the project. Finally, the attraction to U of M was heightened by the possibility (later confirmed) that the files of the Truth and Reconciliation Commission would be deposited there.

Although the committee was unanimous in the decision to deposit the collection at the University of Manitoba Archives for the reasons outlined above, the issue of accessibility is a residual concern. Non–U of M students, and in particular, inner-city residents, will not have easy access to the materials. Indeed, most will likely be unaware of its existence. This concern will be addressed in part by the development of a course related to the project to be offered at the University of Winnipeg Merchants Corner Campus, located in Winnipeg's North End where several of the institutions discussed in the book are situated. Students will be required to visit the U of M collection as part of the course.

Once the location decision had been made, the project underwent another transformation, bringing Shelley Sweeney, the Head of the U of M Archives into the research project. She was joined by Tom Nesmith and Greg Bak of the Archival Studies Program and Jesse Boiteau who was already involved in the project. Archival Studies graduate Sarah Story, who had experience working on archival matters as an intern at the Nelson Mandela Centre of Memory in Johannesburg, South Africa was also hired. These new additions considerably expanded the expertise as well as skilled labour available. Subsequently, Jim Sinclair of the Indian and Métis Friendship Centre (IMFC) worked to secure Canada Works summer employment money to hire two undergraduate Indigenous students—Charlotte Nelson and Kerri Johnston—to work on the paper files of the IMFC. Yet another Indigenous student, Chrystal Kakekagumick, assisted the project in processing files held by the Aboriginal Council of Winnipeg.

The Letter of Understanding

Once the archival destination was determined and materials were ready for deposit, it was necessary to have a clear written agreement laying out the terms by which the materials would be held by the university. While the agreement between the advisory committee and the university archivist, that the university would hold the materials under its stewardship, was pretty straightforward, it was difficult for the two parties to arrive at a mutually acceptable letter of understanding for those supplying material to easily comprehend and sign. The university's standard Deed of Gift Agreement is three-and-a-half pages long without signatures or the list of items "donated." It is both unwieldy and inappropriate. It is wordy and full of legalese that laypeople would find hard to follow. It deals with "property" and its valuation and the charitable tax receipts that might flow to "donors" under the Income Tax Act. More importantly, it states that "The Donor hereby gifts, assigns and transfers all of the Donor's right, title, and interest in and to the Property, to the university, for its own use absolutely, subject only to the terms of this Deed," which hardly suggests a collaborative arrangement.[17]

In response to these concerns about the standard Deed of Gift Agreement, the university drafted a new letter of understanding. This was a much shorter (half a page), more intelligible, and more accessible document. It dropped references to "donors" replacing them with "stewards" and provided for the university to act as a new steward of the materials. It stated that the university would "respect Indigenous archival principles." It also stated that the university was not obligated to retain the materials indefinitely but may transfer them "according to standard archival principles" to another archive "if they feel the records would be more appropriate to be housed at another facility." Members of the advisory committee felt, however, that this draft was still deficient in a number of ways. For instance, in the event that the university wished to transfer the materials outside of its stewardship, there was no provision for consultation with the original stewards who donated the documents and no suggestion that the transfer would be governed by Indigenous archival principles. There was also no attempt to define what "standard Indigenous archival principles" might look like. After much discussion, the advisory committee recommended that the transfer paragraph be reworded as follows:

> The University may transfer or dispose of the Materials according to standard Indigenous archival principles such as the Society of American Archivists' Protocols for Native American Archival materials. For example, after consulting with the steward(s), the University

17 University of Manitoba policy, donating to to the archives. https://libguides.lib.umanitoba.ca/archives/donating

may transfer a portion or all of the Materials to another archive if they feel records would be more appropriately housed at the other facility.[18]

The lawyers for the university would not accept this wording. Even so, the redrafted letter of understanding with its emphasis on stewardship and Indigenous archival principles represented a major step forward for the university and, according to the University Head Archivist, is probably unique in Canada (see appendix 4).

Celebration Feast

The advisory committee felt it was important to celebrate the completion of the project by inviting those interviewed and those who had donated papers or worked on the project to a feast. The idea to celebrate was inspired in part by Kathy Mallett, who noted in her interview, "I wish we had more time to celebrate changing the system ... and to celebrate and acknowledge the people you are working with."[19]

The gathering was held on October 22, 2013, at Circle of Life Thunderbird House in Winnipeg, and the meal was catered by Neechi Foods, an Indigenous workers' co-op. Invitations were sent to approximately 100 people and some eighty people attended. In preparation for the meeting, Darryl Nepinak produced a film which drew on six of the interviews (those with Doris Young, George Munroe, Wayne Helgason, Kathy Mallett, Vern Morrissette, and Larry Morrissette), and

18 This paragraph contains an important footnote about Indigenous archival principles that reads as follows: "Canada does not have a set of protocols for archiving Indigenous materials and badly needs one. Shelley Sweeney has been developing an Indigenous Archiving Policy for the University of Manitoba based on the Aboriginal and Torres Strait Islander Data Archive (ATSIDA) Protocols of Australia, which are grounded in respect, trust and engagement (http://www.atsida.edu.au/protocols/atsida/principles)."

19 Quoted in Darryl Nepinak, "Preserving the History of Aboriginal Institutional Development," published on the Canadian Centre for Policy Alternatives YouTube Channel, October 21, 2013, https://www.youtube.com/watch?v=EJAs8-x8a1I.

in which he also interviewed the principal investigators and the head archivist at the U of M. This short film was shown at the feast and was very well received.[20] An archival display was prepared by Sarah Story, one of the graduate archival students, and invited speakers included representatives of, both, Aboriginal youth (male and female) and Aboriginal elders. Local press reported on the project, the feast, and the video, describing those interviewed for the project as "Aboriginal trailblazers."[21] The news story included a photo at the gathering of Chief Jim Bear (Brokenhead First Nation), Jim Sinclair (executive director of the Indian and Métis Friendship Centre), Lorne Keeper (executive director of the First Nations Education Resource Centre), and Dan Highway (Indigenous activist, role model, and residential school survivor).

Challenges of the Project

The main challenges of the project concerned both time and money. The advisory committee met regularly, and its work was quite demanding on all members. The agendas were substantial, and at every meeting, practical decisions had to be made, such as selecting people and organizations to be interviewed. Members were tasked with seeking out participant contact information, hiring staff to do the interviewing, overseeing staff reporting on progress, conducting pre-video interviews, reviewing videos, and planning for the feast to wind up the project. The committee also had to deal with any personnel issues that arose. While much of the work was handled by the investigators, all members of the advisory committee were heavily involved. There was no remuneration for this work, and the Indigenous members participated out of dedication to the project.

Conducting the interviews and contacting organizations for their paper records also took time. Organizing and finalizing over forty

20 Quoted in ibid.

21 Jared Story, "Video Project Tells Story of Trailblazers," *The Times (Winnipeg)*, October 30, 2013, 9.

videotaping sessions took much longer than originally anticipated, and this, in turn, raised the cost of the project in terms of wages for those conducting the interviews. This heightened the second challenge, which was a financial one. Initially, the money to hire researchers came from SSHRC grants through the MRA. This was insufficient for the scale of video interviews. The project relied heavily, therefore, on Evelyn Peters' CRC funding, which covered most of the labour of the interviewers and the videographer. The U of M Office of Indigenous Achievement also funded one of the Aboriginal researchers. The Faculty of Graduate Studies at the U of M generously funded one of the MA students in the Archival Studies program. The wind-up feast was funded partly by the U of M, partly by the U of W, and partly by community-based social organization the Community Education Development Association of Winnipeg (CEDA). So funding was a patchwork quilt, and keeping the project going was quite a demanding endeavour. Organizing the interviews was also challenging given the sheer number and the various stages through which each interview and subsequent edits had to pass. Some of those on the list to be interviewed no longer lived in Winnipeg and hooking up with them was complicated.

Impressions and Legacy of the Project

The overwhelming impression we are left with after the completion of the Indigenous Archives Project is that it is a source of great pride to the Indigenous participants on the advisory committee, to the Indigenous people interviewed, and to the Indigenous community as a whole. The interviews highlight the lack of supports for Indigenous people coming to Winnipeg as early as the 1950s, and the creative ways in which people banded together to help with the transition to urban life. A myriad of formal institutions developed to meet the diverse and growing needs of the Indigenous urban community. The Winnipeg Indian and Métis Friendship Centre founded in 1958 played a very important role here, and it was also the breeding ground for several other important institutional developments, such as the Main Street Project, the introduction of Aboriginal court translators, and the establishment of hospital cultural interpreters.[22] The video interviews provide a comprehensive account of subsequent institutional developments in Winnipeg and the rich diversity of approaches followed in fields of child welfare, women's issues, education, employment, training, and economic development. The project recorded that by 2013, some 200 Indigenous institutions had existed or were currently active.[23] This rich institutional development "is the success side and it really needs to be told because it's an important part of what is happening in Winnipeg today."[24]

Conclusions

The success of this project is a testimony to the foresight of the Social Sciences and Humanities Research Council (SSHRC) to support joint community-academic research through Community University Research Alliance (CURA) grants and later Partnership Grants. Without this central institutional financial support, this project would not have been possible. Additionally, the flexibility of financial support provided by Evelyn Peters, through the Tri-Council funded CRC, allowed the project to evolve organically. We were fortunate, therefore, in having these two flexible sources of funds available for the research.

While much has been accomplished, more remains to be done. Some important Indigenous pathbreakers were not interviewed, mainly because they live outside of Winnipeg. New leaders and institution builders are emerging as every year goes by. And much more

22 Darrell Chippeway quoted in Sanders, "Putting Together a Piece of History," March 4, 2013, A6.

23 Chippeway, *A Report*, 1.

24 Evelyn Peters in CBC News, "Winnipeg's Urban Aboriginal History Being Pieced Together," Video, March 4, 2013, http://www.cbc.ca/news/canada/manitoba/winnipeg-s-urban-aboriginal-history-being-pieced-together-1.1398000.

needs to be done to collect and preserve the paper and digital records of Indigenous institutions. This book aims to fill some of these gaps. The researchers and videographers experienced in this type of work are on the ground and the archival arrangements are now in place.

The Indigenous Archives Project inspired this book as well as the development of a university course to be offered at the University of Winnipeg through the Department of Urban and Inner-City Studies. The course will bring students to the University of Manitoba Archives to learn more about Indigenous activists who led the development of important Indigenous-led institutions in the city of Winnipeg. We hope that offering students access to this history as told by Indigenous people who were involved will not only inspire Indigenous youth to "be proud of who you are and get involved," but also to inspire them to document their activities for generations to follow.[25]

25 Chippeway, *A Report*, 12–13.

Appendix 1: Ethics Approval Document—Indicative List of Questions to Be Asked

Set A—for persons who might be knowledgeable about which institutions exist or existed

Please review this preliminary list of Aboriginal institutional initiatives in Winnipeg and comment on its completeness.

Are there any other institutions, which are not listed? If so, what are they?

What were the functions of those institutions and who were the key actors?

Do you have contact addresses for the key actors?

Do you know where written records of these institutions might be held and by whom?

Were there suggestions for Aboriginal institutions which never materialized? If so, what were they and who were the key actors?

Do you foresee any problems in our contacting these key actors?

Set B—for people identified as key actors in institutions, which exist or existed

Please describe the nature of your involvement with the institution in question.

What was/is the nature of the institution and what are/were its goals?

Do you know the whereabouts of any documents relating to the formation, operation evaluation or, if it no longer exists, the closure of the institution?

These documents could include aims and objectives, legal documents, minutes of meetings, funding requests, ads for public meetings, presentations to government or other bodies, financial reports, contributions to public debate, record of accomplishments, etc.

Who else involved in the project might have kept records and how might they be reached?

Would there be any problems making these records available publicly?

If written records do not exist, or if they are deficient, would you be prepared to contribute orally to recreating or creating such records?

Set C—for key actors where written records are non-existent or deemed deficient

Please describe the nature, purpose and origin of the initiative.

What major issues was the initiative designed to address and why was it deemed necessary?

What problems did it face and how did it attempt to overcome them?

How was it funded?

Who was involved in the initiative? Were people paid or were they volunteers?

What was your role in the initiative?

What were the accomplishments of the initiative?

If it no longer exists, why is this?

Why were no records kept or, if they were, why were they deficient?

What is your evaluation of the contribution of this initiative to improving the lives of Aboriginal people in Winnipeg?

Do you wish to be quoted in any write-up on this initiative?

Are there other sources which might add to your recollection?

Appendix 2: Suggested Questions for Key Aboriginal Contacts

Could you please describe when you came to Winnipeg and under what circumstances?

Did coming to Winnipeg represent a clean break with your home community or have you remained in contact since? If you have remained in contact, please describe your relationship over the years with your home community.

Where did you do your schooling and, if you feel able and willing to share this, what is your assessment of your schooling experience?

Did you return to school in your adult years and if so, why, where and with what effect?

What facilities and supports were there for Aboriginal newcomers to Winnipeg when you and your family arrived?

Could you describe the organizations with which you have been involved since coming to Winnipeg, their purpose, funding sources and role in the community. Please describe the role(s) you played in developing these organizations. How would you assess the experience(s) and the performance and contribution of these organizations?

How do you see Aboriginal organizations which now exist in Winnipeg? Do they cater for the main needs of Aboriginal people? Are there any gaps?

What role have Aboriginal women played in developing Aboriginal organizations in Winnipeg?

How would you describe the principles which have governed your activities in the community?

In the Aboriginal community there appear to be quite diverse approaches to community economic development, for instance the collectivist approach of Neechi versus the more private enterprise oriented approach of Stan Fulham. What would be your views on these different approaches? Are there other approaches you would recommend?

How have your children and grandchildren fared in Winnipeg over the years?

Would you say that because of Aboriginal initiatives, Winnipeg is a better place for Aboriginal people to live than it was when you first arrived? If so, why and how? If not, why and how?

What would you recommend needs to be done by contemporary Aboriginal youth to improve the lives of Aboriginal people in Winnipeg?

Appendix 3: Initial List of Potential Interviewees

Bartlett, Marileen
Bear, Jim
Black, Darlene
Bruce, Barbara
Bruce, Lucille
Callahan, Ann
Champagne, Louise
Chaske, Ivy
Chippeway, Louise
Courchene, Mary
Cowan, Elaine
Daniels, Dennis
Fontaine, Janet
Fontaine, Phil
Friesen, Lena
Guilbault, Mary
Helgason, Wayne
Highway, Dan
Hill, Josie
Jackson, Tom
Johnston, Damion
Keeper, Cyril
Keeper, Joe
Laramee, Myra
Lavallee, Jackie
Lavallee, Margaret and Jules
Mallett, Kathy
McCloud, Albert
McKay, Stan
Mead, Thelma
Meadmore, Marion
Mercredi, Ovide
Monkman, Yvonne
Morrissette, Larry
Morrissette, Vern
Munroe, George
Murdock, Ruth
Nepinak, Clarence
Robertson, Don
Roesler, Francis
Schoffly, Art
Shead, Bill
Sinclair, Murray
Spillett, Leslie
Westasacoot, Jim
Young, Doris
Zaharia, Flora

Appendix 4: Letter of Understanding

I/We ____

am/are the recognized steward(s) of the material to be transferred, or represent the steward(s), and have full authority to enter into this agreement. This transfer is not subject to the conditions of any other agreements, or to the consent of any other person or persons.

I/we agree to transfer and assign all rights to the outlined materials (see attached transfer schedule) (the "Materials") to the University of Manitoba Archives & Special Collections, (the "University") which will act as steward of these materials for the use absolutely of the larger community subject to this letter of understanding.

Any desired copyrights and/or access restrictions must be agreed upon between the person(s) transferring and the University of Manitoba Archives & Special Collections prior to the transfer.

It is the University's intention to archive and hold these Materials in order to preserve them, yet the University is not obligated to retain the Materials indefinitely. The University may transfer or dispose of the Materials according to standard archival principles. For example, the University may transfer a portion or all of the Materials to another archive if they feel the records would be more appropriate to be housed at the other facility.

The steward(s) will protect the University so that the University will not be held liable for any claims relating to the steward's/stewards' stewardship of the Materials and right to transfer the Materials to the University.

Steward's Name (please print):

____

Address:

____

Telephone ______________________

(Organisation) ____________________

Date _______________ Signature __________________

University of Manitoba
Per: ___________________________

Schedule
Transfer agreement

From _____________________ to the University of Manitoba

The following records are transferred to the University of Manitoba as of (date): ______________________________________

1.	6.
2.	7.
3.	8.
4.	9.
5.	10.

____

(Witness signature)

____

(Steward's signature)

Steward's Name: ________________________________

Bibliography

Boiteau, Jesse. "Co-curation and Participatory Archives." Presentation to symposium, *I Have Never Forgotten His Words... Talking about Indigenous Archives*. The Institute for the Humanities, University of Manitoba, October 5, 2013.

CBC News. "Winnipeg's Urban Aboriginal History Being Pieced Together." Video. March 4, 2013. http://www.cbc.ca/news/canada/manitoba/winnipeg-s-urban-aboriginal-history-being-pieced-together-1.1398000.

Chippeway, Darrell. *A Report on Preserving the History of Aboriginal Institutional Development in Winnipeg Project*. Winnipeg: Manitoba Research Alliance, 2013.

Indian and Métis Friendship Centre. *History of the Winnipeg Indian and Métis Friendship Centre, 1958–1983: 25 Years of Service and Development in the Winnipeg Community*. Winnipeg: IMFC, 1983.

Loxley, John. *Aboriginal, Northern, and Community Economic Development: Papers and Retrospectives*. Winnipeg: ARP Books, 2010.

Loxley, John, and Evelyn Peters. "Preserving the History of Indigenous Institutional Development in Winnipeg: Research Driven by the Community." In *Practising Community-Based Participatory Research: Stories of Engagement, Empowerment and Mobilization*, edited by Shauna MacKinnon. 193-212.Vancouver: UBC-Purich Press, 2018.

Loxley, John, Bernie Wood, Louise Champagne, E.J. Fontaine, and Charles Scribe. *Aboriginal People in the Winnipeg Economy: Case Study*. Royal Commission on Aboriginal Peoples, Ottawa, Volume 5, 1996. (Appendix B). http://www.collectionscanada.gc.ca/webarchives/20071124124835/; http://www.ainc-inac.gc.ca/ch/rcap/sg/ska5d_e.html (page discontinued).

Nepinak, Darryl. "Preserving the History of Aboriginal Institutional Development in Winnipeg." Published on the Canadian Centre for Policy Alternatives YouTube Channel. October 21, 2013. https://www.youtube.com/watch?v=EJAs8-x8a1I.

Peters, Evelyn. "'The Two Major Living Realities': Urban Services Needs of First Nations Women in Canadian Cities," in *Gendering the City: Women, Boundaries and Visions of Urban Life*, edited by Kristine B. Miranne and Alma H. Young. Lanham, MD: Rowman and Littlefield, 2000.

Sanders, Carol. "Putting Together a Piece of History." *Winnipeg Free Press*, March 4, 2013.

Silver, Jim. *Solutions That Work: Fighting Poverty in Winnipeg.* Winnipeg: Canadian Centre for Policy Alternatives-Manitoba; Winnipeg: Fernwood Publishing, 2000.

Stinnett, Graham. *Urban Aboriginal Organizations.* Report on Research Progress, November 24, 2008.

Story, Jared. "Video Project Tells Story of Trailblazers." *The Times (Winnipeg)*, October 30, 2013.

Chapter 2

Establishing and Indigenizing the Indian and Métis Friendship Centre:

An Incubator for Indigenous Activism[1]

Shauna MacKinnon and Kathy Mallett

> A friend of mine found the Friendship Centre...There were socials there every Saturday night so that's where we would go. It was a good place. It was a gathering place of Aboriginal people...When I first came to Winnipeg, I felt a lot of shame about being Aboriginal, but I think by becoming involved with the Indian and Métis Friendship Centre and Club 376 and seeing Aboriginal role models and Aboriginal leaders, I was transformed. I finally became proud of who I was as an Aboriginal person.[2]—Louise Chippeway

Friendship Centres emerged in response to the postwar migration of Indigenous peoples to urban areas.[3] Established in 1959, the Winnipeg

1 The authors had several conversations with Flora Zaharia and thank her for her input and review.
2 Louise Chippeway, interview by Darrell Chippeway, 2013. Recording at the University of Manitoba Archives, Winnipeg, MB.
3 Will Langford, "Friendship Centres in Canada, 1959–1977," *The American Indian Quarterly*, 40, no. 1, (Winter 2016): 1-37

Indian and Métis Friendship Centre (IMFC) was the first Friendship Centre in Canada. It was initially established to provide "guidance and counselling" for Indigenous people living in the city, but it has always been far more than a service organization.[4] The IMFC has been described by several individuals involved in its early days as an epicentre of Indigenous activism. In a 2019 article in the *Winnipeg Free Press*, Niigaan Sinclair notes that "without it, there would be little of the economic and social development in the North End and much of the rest of the city we know today."[5]

The history of Winnipeg's IMFC is rich and complex. In this chapter we aim to chronicle the early years of its development from the perspective of the Indigenous people who were involved. Many of those interviewed for the Preserving Aboriginal Institutional History in Winnipeg project (Chapter 1) refer to the Indian and Métis Friendship Centre as the place where it all began for them. Drawing from those interviews, this chapter tells the story of Indigenous leadership in the development of the IMFC through the voices of those who were involved from the beginning through to the early 1980s.

The IMFC was first and foremost intended to be a meeting place and service provider for Indigenous people in Winnipeg. The services it offered evolved considerably after it opened its doors in downtown Winnipeg. It began with a fairly small, accessible storefront space at 376 Donald Street that included a few offices, a lounge, a recreation room, a kitchenette, and a craft room.[6] With support from her assistant Dorothy McKay, the first executive director Joan Adams provided counselling and referral services. In addition to being a friendly and welcoming place where people would visit over tea and bannock, staff

4 Indian and Métis Friendship Centre, *History of the Winnipeg Indian and Métis Friendship Centre 1958–1983; 25 Years of Service and Development in the Winnipeg Community* (Winnipeg: IMFC, 1983), 3.

5 Niigaan Sinclair, "With a Proud Past, Friendship Centre to Rise Again," *Winnipeg Free Press*, June 12, 2019.

6 Indian and Métis Friendship Centre, *History*.

and volunteers provided people with assistance finding jobs, housing, and medical services. Responding to a growing need to support Indigenous people involved in the criminal justice system, Alex Daniels was hired in 1962 as the first court worker. When he left in 1963, he was replaced by Earl Duncan, and in 1964, Vera Richard was hired as a court worker to support women, youth, and families.[7] The number of services and people involved expanded over the years, and by 1983 it was a well-established service provider to Indigenous people receiving funding from the federal and provincial governments.

Although it was established to provide services for Indigenous people, many involved in the Friendship Centre were also front and center in the resistance movements that emerged in the 1960s and continued through the 1970s. Indigenous activists of that era commonly attribute the IMFC's Club 376 as central to their politicization and mobilization. The activity around the IMFC also led to the development of Indigenous-led institutions and influenced a number of Indigenous youths who went on to become effective community leaders.

Although the idea of creating the IMFC was driven by Indigenous peoples, Winnipeg's community-based, non-profit, non-Indigenous-led Welfare Planning Council of Greater Winnipeg (WPC) played a prominent role in the early days. The IMFC was initially led by an all-white board. The IMFC was established following the Indian and Métis Conference in 1958, an annual event organized by the WPC "to research and discuss the needs of Aboriginal people in the city."[8] The Indigenous activists who formed the Urban Indian Association that collaborated with the WPC conference planning committee as a means of moving their agenda forward, were well aware that members

7 Ibid.

8 Leslie Hall, "The Early History of the Winnipeg Indian and Métis Friendship Centre, 1951–1968," in *Prairie Metropolis: New Essays on Winnipeg Social History*, ed. Esyllt Jones and Gerald Friesen (Winnipeg: University of Manitoba Press, 2009), 228.

of the WPC conference planning committee "were all-white, hardly any Indian participation and these are the guys that talked about Indian problems."[9]

The "Urban Indian Problem"

The annual Indian and Métis Conference was organized by the WPC, which had been established as the Winnipeg Council of Social Agencies in 1919. The non-profit organization changed its name to the Welfare Planning Council in 1947 and later became the Social Planning Council of Winnipeg. The mandate of the Welfare Planning Council was to conduct research on social issues and to mobilize support for services to address social needs. In the early 1950s, the WPC established an Indian and Métis Committee to investigate the needs of Indigenous residents of Winnipeg. The Indigenous population in Winnipeg was growing; poverty, unemployment and lack of housing were the reality for far too many Indigenous people, and they were not being adequately served.

The Indian and Métis Conference was initially structured like an academic conference, with a heavy emphasis on academic research papers and presentations by government officials. The emphasis was on what was commonly described at that time as the "urban Indian problem." Leslie Hall notes that the majority of reports on the conferences that survive in archival records, newspapers, and interviews suggest that Indigenous voices were not central in the deliberations.[10] Joyce Meyer of the Winnipeg Tribune quoted an "Indian representative" at the 1959 Indian and Métis Conference saying, "I think the Welfare Council is doing its best—and in good faith. They are always ready to listen ... but maybe next year they should leave a few gaps in the agenda in case Indians have something to say. This year there were no gaps at all."[11] George Munroe echoes this observation in a 2013 interview

9 Marion Meadmore, interview by Darrell Chippeway and Louise Chippeway, 2013, recording at the University of Manitoba Archives, Winnipeg, MB.

10 Hall, "The Early History," 228.

11 Ibid.

with Darrell and Louise Chippeway and Larry Morissette. Munroe led efforts to establish the Indian and Métis Friendship Centre and later to transform it as an Indigenous-led institution. He recalls he and Flora Zaharia having an "epiphany" at one of the conferences after the IMFC was established. They decided they were no longer willing to allow non-Indigenous people to speak on their behalf. That, he says, was a pivotal moment that led them to organize to take control of the IMFC, which was run at that time by a non-Indigenous board of directors.

"Changes happen when the grassroots people get involved"[12]

In response to the question of what led himself, Flora, and others to no longer accept their roles as Indigenous advisors to the all-white board, Munroe says,

> When you're under a lot of oppression and under a lot of suppression by the society you get really angry. So, one of the things you do is you lash out at the people that are oppressing you. But you also look at, raise some questions about, why these things are taking place—why are we without a voice? Why are we at the bottom rung of the economic, social, and political ladder in the province? And why aren't people taking our concerns and our issues seriously? Because those Indian and Métis conferences were really a showpiece for, not for us, but for the bleeding hearts for [lack of] a better term, to make them feel good that they were doing something about our problems ... and really, nothing came of those conferences except people feeling good about themselves.

The Urban Indian Association

At the same time that non-Indigenous people were talking about "Indian problems," Indigenous activists were organizing. In 1955, a small

12 George Munroe, interview by Darrell Chippeway, Louise Chippeway and Larry Morrissette, 2013, recording at the University of Manitoba Archives and Special Collections, Winnipeg, MB.

group—including Marion Meadmore, who was a university student at the time—formed the Urban Indian Association (UIA) to discuss the needs of Indigenous people in the city and how to best respond to these needs. This group worked independently of the WPC until 1958 when its members attended that year's Indian and Métis Conference and agreed to a partnership that would result in the creation of the Indian and Métis Friendship Centre. Marion Meadmore reflects back on that time: "The community started doing things together and one of the things we did as a community is, we worked with this white committee that had these annual conferences... So, we began to work with them and between the two of us we started to formulate a concept [that became] the Friendship Centre."[13] The UIA met regularly in each other's homes to research and design plans to address the needs of the Indigenous population. Mary Guilbault and Meadmore spearheaded various independent research efforts to assess the needs of urban Indigenous people as well as to consider what people in other cities were doing to address these needs. According to Guilbault, they wanted to provide a meeting place and assist people in obtaining housing, employment, and health care.[14]

The UIA members participated in the fourth annual Indian and Métis Conference in 1958 where a resolution was made to open a referral agency to provide guidance on matters of employment, housing, education, health, and other community services for Indigenous people moving to the city.[15] Mary Guilbault recalls that the UIA was concerned that the Welfare Council would take control of the Friendship Centre and shape it in the council's image without Indigenous influence. Those concerns turned out to be warranted. The board of directors initially consisted of sixteen non-Indigenous community

13 Marion Meadmore interview by Darrell Chippeway, April 19, 2012. Recording at University of Manitoba Archives and Special Collections, Winnipeg, MB

14 Hall, "The Early History."

15 Indian and Métis Friendship Centre, *History*, 231.

members. Four Indigenous representatives were named to an Indian Advisory Council.

A planning committee was established by the Welfare Planning Council to set up the administration of the Friendship Centre. This committee included four non-Indigenous representatives and four Indigenous representatives—Mary and Ernie Guilbault, Marion Meadmore, and Dorothy Betz. The committee determined that the centre would be run by two, equal but different, governing bodies—the Board of Directors and the Indian Advisory Council (IAC). A third, subsidiary group of thirty people who represented various "community organisations which have an interest in the welfare of Indian and Métis in the city," formed a group called the Advisory Committee which provided additional advice to the board during the first year of operation.[16] The role of the board of directors was to administer public funds, determine policy, hire staff, appoint committees, and generally supervise the administrative affairs of the centre. Although there were many discussions about including Indigenous people in the administration of the Friendship Centre, it continued to be dominated by non-Indigenous people until 1972.

Archival documents describe the IAC as having been established to ensure Indigenous people had a role in the administration of the IMFC. However, it is clear from the Indigenous people involved that this division was questioned early on. The IAC met independently from the board meetings, had fundraising responsibilities, and designed and implemented programming at the centre.[17] Archival documents note that the board of directors and the executive director relied on the IAC to identify needs and suggest appropriate programs. The board believed that the "success of the Centre is due in part at least, to the fact that many Indian people feel a responsibility for planning and carrying out projects and programme at the centre and we suggest that only

16 Welfare Council of Greater Winnipeg, "Indian and Métis conference 6th Annual Proceedings" as cited in Hall, "The Early History", 232.

17 Hall, "The Early History," 232.

when the Indian people themselves are involved in a responsible way, can a service for Indians be effective."[18]

However, only the board held decision-making powers. Marion Meadmore explains it this way:

> That original committee that were in control of the Friendship Centre... they didn't really trust Indian people to be in control. Appointing us to an advisory committee [IAC] was their way of bringing us in because they didn't think we could be on the board, and it wasn't until eight years later that I became president of the board, but we deliberately tried to assume control...[19]

The IAC consisted of twelve people elected by the IMFC membership. The constitution stated that the purpose of the IAC was to

> involve people of Indian origin in helping to plan activities and programs relating to the centre, such programs include activities of a social, recreational, educational and welfare nature; act in an advisory capacity to both the staff and Board of the Centre; provide one means of leadership development among people of Indian origin; draw up and enforce regulations concerning behaviours at the centre; raise funds, as deemed advisable, to be used at the discretion of the council; provide speakers to speak on the work of the centre and matters relating to people of Indian origin for church and community groups; seek to pass on to the community at large a true picture of people of Indian origin.[20]

Flora Zaharia became a member of the IAC in 1962 and expressed concerns about the inequity of having Indigenous people relegated to the IAC rather than having a prominent place on the board. In a 2013

18 Quoted in ibid.

19 Marion Meadmore interview by Darrell Chippeway, April 19, 2012. Recording at University of Manitoba Archives and Special Collections, Winnipeg, MB

20 Quoted in Hall, "The Early History," 233.

interview with Darrell Chippeway and Larry Morissette, Flora Zaharia describes having attended her first few meetings sitting with the other Indigenous IAC members and wondering why the white board was meeting separately from the IAC and making all the decisions. She wondered, "How come they meet up there? What about these intelligent people?" She finally got the courage to ask Executive Director Joan Adams, "Why is it that the board members are all non-native? I feel there are people here that could do the job quite well." Adams responded, "I don't know." This would eventually change.

As a member organization of the WPC, many of the people involved in the IMFC continued their association with the WPC through the annual Indian and Métis Conference. Initial funding for the centre was provided in the form of three grants, the first from the Winnipeg Foundation for $3500, the second and third from the Province of Manitoba and the federal government's Citizenship Branch, each contributing $4000 per year for a two-year trial period. After the successful two-year trial period, the IMFC's funding continued to come from assorted limited-term grants from the federal, provincial, and municipal governments, and various community agencies. The centre continued to assist Indigenous people who were new to the city adapt to urban life; to inform the larger community about the problems facing Indigenous people in the city; and to work with community groups, churches, and the government to provide improved access to health and welfare services.[21] Despite receiving funds from the federal and provincial governments, which generally supported assimilation, Guilbault says, "it was always known that the Friendship Centre would be used as a steppingstone into society for everything—that [the centre] would be a learning place... We never intended to have the Friendship Centre be used as a place of assimilation."[22]

21 Hall, "The Early History," 231.

22 Ibid.

Although the narrative of the board suggested an understanding that colonial assimilationist policies were deeply damaging and that new approaches were needed, non-Indigenous board members continued to see fit to lead the IMFC and focus on the "Indian problem."[23] This was not left unchallenged. Métis WPC board member and provincial civil servant John Lagassé was highly critical of traditional social services. He called for a community-development approach as a way of bringing about self-directed social and economic progress. Lagassé believed in focusing on the strengths of the community and in prioritizing cultural reclamation and practice. His ideas became central to the programming at the IMFC.[24]

Initially located at 376 Donald Street, the IMFC would relocate several times as it expanded. In 1967 the IMFC relocated to a larger space at 73 Princess Avenue and then to 590 Main Street. In 1992 it relocated to 465 Alexander Avenue and in 1992 to 45 Robinson Avenue. It later established the Native Club on River Avenue, providing sport and recreation activities for Indigenous youth. All the while it maintained it aims and objectives to "assist Indian and part Indian newcomers in the adjustment to urban life; inform the community about the problems of Indians in the city and to take action in resolving the problems; plan with government and voluntary health and welfare services, churches, and other community groups to improve service to newcomers of Indian origin."[25] Created to support a growing Aboriginal and Métis population in Winnipeg and in response to the need for specialized social and economic services, the IMFC developed and supported many programs and services. The IMFC also acted as a cultural centre

23 Marion Meadmore interview by Darrell Chippeway, April 19, 2012. Recording at University of Manitoba Archives and Special Collections, Winnipeg, MB.

24 Toby Morantz, "Reflections on the Annual Manitoba Indian and Métis Conferences of the Early 1960s," *Papers of the First Algonquian Conference*, 40 (2008).

25 Indian and Métis Friendship Centre, *History*.

and "aspired to empower the community by taking action on issues affecting Aboriginal peoples."[26] In 1972 it became a member of The National Association of Friendship Centres, the unifying representative body for the friendship centre movement.

In addition to providing services to Indigenous people, the Indian and Métis Friendship Centre is widely described by Indigenous people actively engaged in resistance and development during the 1960s, '70s and '80s as being influential in their personal and political lives. Descriptions of the IMFC range from a "friendly place to go for tea and bannock" to a place where Indigenous youth were "conscientized and politicized."[27] Early organizers at the IMFC Club 376 and those who frequented and entertained at its Purple Pit included people who would later become prominent leaders, including people like Ovide Mercredi (Assembly of First Nations Grand Chief 1991 to 1997), actor and musician Tom Jackson, Marion Meadmore (Canada's first female First Nations lawyer), and many others. Cyril Keeper worked at the IMFC in the 1960s and was later elected as a Member of Parliament (MP). George Munroe was a founder, long-time activist and organizer, and the executive director of the IMFC from 1969 to 1974. He was the first Indigenous person to be elected to Winnipeg City Council (1972–1974). Many others went on to be prominent leaders in the community.

Club 376 is described as "one of the most successful ventures in the history of the IMFC."[28] George Munroe describes Club 376—which took its name from its address on Donald Street at the time—as "a group of politically engaged Indigenous youth who were influenced a great deal by the civil rights and Red Power movements in the United States."[29] Club 376 was "the lightning rod for all the changes that took place, including the Manitoba Métis Federation, the Manitoba

26 Ibid.

27 Flora Zaharia, interview by Darrell Chippeway and Larry Morrissette, 2013, recording at the University of Manitoba Archives, Winnipeg, MB.

28 Indian and Métis Friendship Centre, *History*, 7.

29 Humalajoki, "Yours in Indian Unity," 183-198.

Indian Brotherhood, national and provincial associations and other Friendship Centres…"[30]

Munroe recalls the late 1960s as being a critical time of consciousness-raising and "agitation" that led to a sea of change, and those involved with Club 376 were fully engaged. He also critically reflects back on some of their accomplishments. 1967 was a particularly pivotal year that was the beginning of significant change. The IMFC organized a conference at the Marlborough Hotel in Winnipeg, a conference he describes as being the "catalyst for two vital organizations that would serve the political needs of the Métis an Indian People." This included the Manitoba Métis Federation (MMF) and the Manitoba Indian Brotherhood (MIB). For some, it marked the beginning of a divide in the Indigenous community.[31] Louise Chippeway fondly remembers the early days when "we were still a group of Aboriginal people…We believed in ourselves as Aboriginal people and yeah, we were still one. It didn't matter what was happening at the political level. Yeah, we were still one group of people and there was no differentiation at that time between Status or Non-Status, or Métis, or Inuit."[32]

Munroe describes being one member of a small group that "wrote up the resolution to form the MMF." Once established, it was officially incorporated as a political organization in 1967. He describes having mixed feelings about it as he believes it marked the beginning of a more divisive time. He explains, "As soon as money came into the picture then people that you never suspected to have any Aboriginal ancestry were jumping out of the bloody woodwork 'cause there was money involved. And I think money has been our curse ever since, because it's just divided the community."[33] Reflecting on the best

30 George Munroe, interview by Darrell Chippeway, September 17 2013 Recording at the University of Manitoba Archives and Special Collections. Winnipeg, MB.

31 Ibid.

32 Chippeway, interview.

33 Munroe, interview.

of times when things were less complicated, he and others describe the IMFC as being inclusive of anyone who identified as Indigenous. IMFC founder and organizer Mary Guilbault recalls the inclusivity of the IMFC as being critically important: "It wasn't important because Mary Guilbault thought it was important, it was important to think that people were not excluded [and] their children in years to come would always have a place to go to take programs and a special place to vent or whatever."[34] Guilbault's daughter Myra Laramee echoes the importance of the IMFC for her as a child: "The Friendship Centre raised me; those old people were my elders. But one of the things that I observed, they never saw themselves challenged, they always saw an opportunity. So, everything that I saw them do was solution based, it wasn't misery based."[35]

From "Indian Problems" to Indigenous-led Solutions

Although it took some time, Indigenous people eventually took control over the IMFC. By 1968, it was governed by an all-Indigenous board of directors. As described by George Munroe, Marion Meadmore, Mary Guilbault, Flora Zaharia and others—there came a time when they were no longer willing to accept non-Indigenous people defining Indigenous problems and dictating how to solve them.

George Munroe recalls the pivotal moment when things began to change:

> We had this thing at the Royal Alexander Hotel called the Indian and Métis Conference... Social workers, the clergy and government officials would invite all these Aboriginal people to come in from across the country, the province. We'd sit down and then they would, they would do all the talking while we sat back. And one day—I think it

34 Mary Guilbault, interview by Darrell Chippeway, Louise Chippeway and Myra Laramee, 2013, recording at the University of Manitoba Archives, Winnipeg, MB.

35 In Guilbault, interview.

> was Mary Guilbault that got us going—we had a group of students, I believe they were from Kelvin High, my memory's a little fuzzy, but they were up there talking on our behalf, and we were sitting around and said "well this is crazy. We can't have people speaking on our behalf." So, I got up there, I had the biggest mouth, so they elected me to go and talk. And we said, "Look we're not going to let anybody else speak on our behalf, so from now on we're going to speak for ourselves." And that really started the whole movement to organize.[36]

Marion Meadmore also recalls finally taking over the board after eight years. She left the IMFC board in 1973 and went on to work for Kinew Housing, an organization that was created by the IMFC (see Chapter 3).

Under the leadership of George Munroe, the IMFC was interested in moving beyond service responses to tackling structural issues that were the cause of their "problems." It also wanted to have greater control over the social and economic matters of Indigenous people living in the city. As described in Chapter 4, the initial idea of Neeginan Centre was the vision of George Munroe and others at the IMFC during his time as executive director. It was adapted in the 1990s by the Aboriginal Council of Winnipeg and IMFC alumni, which included former executive director Mary Richard, which led to the development of the Aboriginal Centre and Circle of Life Thunder Bird House. The IMFC expanded considerably during that period and was a growing force in Winnipeg. George Munroe describes his time as executive director as "turbulent, controversial, exciting, challenging and much more."[37] It was during that period the IMFC established the Native Club on

36 George Munroe, interview by Darrell Chippeway, September 17, 2013. Recording at University of Manitoba Archives and Special Collections, Winnipeg, MB.

37 George Munroe, interview by Darrell Chippeway, September 17, 2013. Recording at University of Manitoba Archives and Special Collections, Winnipeg, MB.

River Avenue, Kinew Housing, the Native Alcoholism and Drug Abuse Council, Main Street Project and several other initiatives.

As George Munroe describes, the original vision of the Neeginan Project was developed from the idea that

> there were so many different little scatterings of groups dealing with the city, the province, and the federal government and all the different departments. We said "why don't we just put everything in one place, have one building? It will be kind of like a multipurpose facility. It will also be a cultural centre where we could bring all these organizations under one roof so that when people needed support or help, they wouldn't have to run around all over hell's half acre... All the services would be in one place. So that was the basic idea behind Neeginan.[38]

Jackson Beardy was commissioned to "do the schematics and the drawings." But despite what Munroe describes as significant "support from the grassroots level," organizations remained divided on the concept, and Neeginan did not come to fruition. He says that some organizations saw it as an attempt by the IMFC "to gain more power" by consolidating everything. From his perspective, "they weren't looking at what this was going to do for the community... they saw it as I would have all this power. They opposed it and fought against it and ultimately, they killed it."[39]

In his interview, George Munroe describes these divisions as an ongoing challenge:

> Even today we've got a proliferation of organizations, and each of them have their own little, little *bailiwick,* and they want to protect it. We tried to get everybody together. We had a meeting a [few] years back where all the organizations including the MMF came together, Billyjo DeLaRonde was president at the time. And we all agreed, we've got to work for the greater good of the community and so therefore we

38 Munroe, interview.

39 Munroe, interview.

> should develop some kind of mechanism whereby we're going to do that. But the way the organizations are set up it is impossible. You just can't do it.[40]

He continues to believe that "if you want change you go to the people, stay away from the organizations. You need to organize the people."[41]

By the 1980s, the Friendship Centre employed more than thirty people and provided services to more than 30,000 citizens annually. It continued its work into the 1990s, moving to 45 Robinson Street in 1992. It remained a hub for Indigenous life in Winnipeg for another twenty-seven years, largely self-supported through fundraising and bingos, with additional support from the Manitoba Association of Friendship Centres. The IMFC continued to operate at 45 Robinson Avenue, however its prominent role in the community had long waned, and, as Niigaan Sinclair explains, the last few years had seen it "fall into political disarray, lose volunteers and partners, and finally close its doors after having its funding suspended by the Manitoba Association of Friendship Centres in 2017."[42]

Tens of thousands of dollars in debt, the IMFC closed its doors in October 2019. However, a new generation of activists are determined to bring the IMFC back to life. Soon after the IMFC closed, two groups—Indigenous Visioning for the North End and the Winnipeg Indigenous Executive Circle—met with representatives from Ma Mawi Wi Chi Itata Centre to establish a new vision. They proposed to the Manitoba Association of Friendship Centres that they re-create the centre either at the existing site or elsewhere. Their proposal to establish the Winnipeg Indigenous Friendship Centre was unanimously approved. Ma Mawi Wi Chi Itata executive director Diane Redsky invited partners to a meeting to "establish the governance" and "oversee the programming" of a new Winnipeg Friendship Centre. A new board

40 Munroe, interview.

41 Munroe, interview.

42 Niigaan, "With a Proud Past."

of directors was established in 2020, and Rachel Sansgreet was hired as the program coordinator. The Winnipeg Indigenous Friendship Centre held its first annual general meeting in June 2021. At the time of writing, planning continues, and the opening date and location of the new centre is yet to be determined.

Bibliography

Chippeway, Louise. Interview by Darrell Chippeway, 2013. Recording at the University of Manitoba Archives, Winnipeg, MB.

Guilbault, Mary. Interview by Darrell Chippeway, Louise Chippeway and Myra Laramee, 2013. Recording at the University of Manitoba Archives, Winnipeg, MB.

Hall, Leslie. "The Early History of the Winnipeg Indian and Métis Friendship Centre, 1951–1968." In *Prairie Metropolis: New Essays on Winnipeg Social History*, edited by Esyllt Jones and Gerald Friesen, 223–241. Winnipeg: University of Manitoba Press, 2009.

Humalajoki, Reetta. "Yours in Idina Unity: Moderate National Indigenous Organisations and the U.S. Canada Border in the Red Power Era. *Comparative American Studies, An International Journal*, 17, 2 (2020): 183-198.

Indian and Métis Friendship Centre. *History of the Winnipeg Indian and Métis Friendship Centre 1958–1983; 25 Years of Service and Development in the Winnipeg Community.* Winnipeg: IMFC, 1983.

Langford, Will. "Friendship Centres in Canada, 1959–1977." *The American Indian Quarterly*, 40, 1 (Winter 2016): 1–37.

Meadmore, Marion. Interview by Darrell Chippeway and Louise Chippeway, 2013. Recording at the University of Manitoba Archives, Winnipeg, MB.

Morantz, Toby. "Reflections on the Annual Manitoba Indian and Métis Conferences of the Early 1960s." *Papers of the First Algonquian Conference*, 40 (2008): 310-325.

Munroe, George. Interview by Darrell Chippeway, Louise Chippeway and Larry Morrissette, 2013. Recording at the University of Manitoba Archives, Winnipeg, MB.

Sinclair, Niigaan. "With a Proud Past, Friendship Centre to Rise Again." *Winnipeg Free Press*, June 12, 2019.

Zaharia, Flora. Interview by Darrell Chippeway and Larry Morrissette, 2013. Recording at the University of Manitoba Archives, Winnipeg, MB.

Chapter 3

Kinew and Payuk:

Leadership in Urban Indigenous Housing

Lawrence Deane and Kathy Mallett

Indigenous housing activism in Winnipeg in the 1970s sparked a movement that spread across Canada. It was in Winnipeg that Indigenous people first developed an initiative to address urban poverty by acquiring suitable housing units, employing Indigenous workers to renovate them, and making these houses available on a subsidized basis for Indigenous families. This chapter traces the development of two innovative Indigenous housing initiatives, Kinew Housing and Payuk Inter-Tribal (Housing) Cooperative. Both projects became role models for Indigenous housing programs across Canada.

Indigenous housing initiatives grew out of a wide range of activism on issues facing Indigenous people in urban areas in the 1960s, '70s, and '80s. As described in Chapter 2, an important starting point for this activism was the Indian and Métis Friendship Centre (IMFC) in Winnipeg.[1] The period from 1950 to 1960 saw a large influx of Indigenous people moving from reserve communities to urban centres.

1 Leslie Hall, "The Early History of the Winnipeg Indian Métis Friendship Centre, 1951–1968," in *Prairie Metropolis: New Essays on Winnipeg Social History*, ed. Esyllt W. Jones and Gerald Friesen (Winnipeg: University of Manitoba Press, 2000).

From 1958 to 1968, the Indigenous population of Winnipeg nearly tripled from 4,700 residents to approximately 12,000.[2] By 1961, Winnipeg had the largest urban Indigenous population in Canada.[3]

Urban areas of the 1960s and '70s were very unwelcoming environments for Indigenous people. A study conducted by the Manitoba Indian Brotherhood in 1971 states,

> The chain of circumstance by which the newly arrived Indian [*sic*] is confronted often irrevocably shackles him [*sic*] to an existence of hopelessness and degradation. We ... contend that the first link in this blighted chain of events is forged by the type of accommodation into which he is thrust ... Why then are Indian people forced to occupy horrendously substandard housing? ... The primary reason is found in the rampant racism directed against the Indian. Although this racism often takes a subtle cast, it is ubiquitous and largely unchecked.[4]

The increased Indigenous presence in Winnipeg, and these conditions of racism, sparked a surge of Indigenous activism. As Chapter 2 describes, the Indian and Métis Friendship Centre represents one of the first comprehensive responses to need.[5] Although primarily a place for recreation and social support, the IMFC developed a variety of social programs to meet specific community needs.[6] Some organizers of the IMFC eventually branched off to develop Kinew Housing. This was Canada's first Indigenous-operated urban housing program.[7] In the first three years of its existence, Kinew

2 Don N. McCaskill, "Migration, Adjustment, and Integration of the Indian into the Urban Environment" (Master's Thesis, Carlton University, 1970), 98.

3 Evelyn J. Peters, "Developing Federal Policy for First Nations People in Urban Areas: 1945–1975" *Canadian Journal of Native Studies* XXI, 1 (2001); Frank Johnston, *Core Area Report: A Reassessment of Conditions in Inner City Winnipeg* (Winnipeg: Institute of Urban Studies, 1979).

4 MIB, *Urban Housing Survey* (Winnipeg: Manitoba Indian Brotherhood, 1971), 7, 22.

5 Hall, "The Early History."

6 Ibid.

7 Marvin Lipman, "Historical Review of CMHC's Urban Native Housing Activity."

("Eagle" in Cree) became a model for three other housing programs across the country. It was also instrumental in the creation of the Native Urban Housing Association of Canada (NUHAC).[8] Activists from this period, such as Marion Meadmore, Mary Guilbault, and Earl Duncan, became role models for a second network of activists who followed a decade later.[9] This second group created a range of programs, such as Ma Mawi Wi Chi Itata Centre, Neechi Foods, Niigaanaki Day Care Centre, and Payuk Inter-Tribal Co-op.[10]

As Chapter 2 describes, the Friendship Centre initially had no Indigenous representation on its board. Indigenous people could only assist in an advisory capacity. The first Indigenous president of the IMFC was Marion Ironquill Meadmore. She spent eight years working with the IMFC before she could finally take this role. After three years as president, Meadmore left to organize Kinew.[11] Because of this experience of exclusion in IMFC, it was highly important to Kinew's organizers that Indigenous people be in full control of the organization. A pattern of stereotyping Indigenous people as incapable of managing formal organizations was to confront organizers repeatedly throughout the history of Indigenous housing activism.

Marion Meadmore was born at Peepeekisis Reserve in Saskatchewan. From the age of seven, she attended residential school. After two years of high school in Birtle, Manitoba, she came to Winnipeg in 1953 to attend university. Meadmore began her university career with an interest in medicine. After she became involved in social change, her focus

8 See Ryan Walker, "The Historical Development of the Canadian Urban Native Housing Program, from Winnipeg to Vancouver" in *Past Matters: Heritage in Planning History—Case Studies from the Pacific Rim*, ed. Caroline L. Miller and Michael Roche (Newcastle-upon-Tyne: Cambridge Scholars Publisher, 2007); Stanley Fulham, A. *In Search of a Future* (Winnipeg: Kinew, 1981).

9 Ivy Chaske, interview by Darrell Chippeway, 2012. Recording at University of Manitoba Archives and Special Collections. Winnipeg, MB.

10 Russ Rothney, interview by Lawrence Deane, 24 November 2021.

11 Marion Meadmore, interview by Darrell Chippeway, 19 April 2012. Recording at University of Manitoba Archives and Special Collections, Winnipeg, MB.

shifted to the study of law. In 1978, Meadmore became Canada's first female Indigenous lawyer.

While attending university, she became aware of Indigenous issues:

> There was a session at the Legislative building in which they were going to be talking about Indian problems, that's the way they addressed things in those days—everything was an Indian problem. And all the white people from the churches, from the social agencies, and volunteers all got around this Indian problem ... So, for some reason I took enough energy and I went down there.[12]

The meeting Meadmore describes here was similar to the Indian and Métis Conferences that were held annually from 1954 to 1958 (as discussed in Chapter 2).[13] She explains,

> And I heard this lady speaking. She was up and she was talking about the poverty in Winnipeg. I couldn't believe the poverty that came from her... her mouth. She told me about living with an alcoholic husband... And she talked about raising four or five kids in her house. Her house didn't have a floor. She almost lived on a mud floor. Her stove was heated using wood... and this was north Winnipeg in '53.[14]

So, Meadmore got involved. She worked with non-Indigenous social workers and church committees. Their initial programs were to provide social support to urban families: "We ... got people together and we held socials and dances, and we introduced this word 'friendship' as being really important."[15]

As Meadmore continued to work at the IMFC, it became more and more apparent that access to decent housing was an important need for Indigenous people coming to the city. Dorothy Betz, who was one of the first court workers at the IMFC, was so frustrated with the lack

12 Ibid.

13 Hall, "The Early History."

14 Meadmore, interview, 2012.

15 Ibid.

of housing that she set up half a dozen bunk beds in her basement to house young people in danger of being charged with vagrancy.[16] Meadmore encountered housing need when she tried to help a friend from university:

> She would phone up and see if a house was available, and I'd drive her there. When we got there, the house was no longer available: a) because she was Native; or b) because she had a child. And this thing kept going on, and I was just ... I couldn't believe things like that happened. And then when she finally got a place, and she's allergic to bed bugs, and behold, it was bed bugs, and she had to get out. So, I thought, gee, that's such trouble for one person ... and exams were coming on ... I thought, somebody's got to do something.[17]

Around the same time, the Manitoba Indian Brotherhood was documenting housing conditions for Indigenous families. The report described leaking toilets, exposed and frayed electrical wiring, rodent infestations, broken windows (covered by poorly fitting plywood), doors through which snow blew into the home in winter, and single pane windows with no outer panes. (Landlords stated that installing storm windows was the tenant's responsibility. No storm windows, however, were provided for the tenants to install.)[18]

In June 1970, Meadmore drew together a group of Indigenous individuals who had been active in various ways on behalf of the community. Each was asked to join because "they were good at getting things done."[19] The group included Norval Desjarlais, Bob Major, Bill Nanowin, and Marvin Hunt. Two non-Indigenous members were George Clarke, a real estate agent who had agreed to train a staff person from Kinew as an agent, and Sidney Schwartz, a lawyer who provided *pro bono* legal advice. In the space of two months, the group drew up

16 Hall, "The Early History."
17 Meadmore, interview, 2012.
18 MIB, *Urban Housing Survey.*
19 Marion Meadmore, interview by Lawrence Deane, 23 February 2022.

its articles of incorporation and registered as a non-profit corporation. Academics who wrote about Kinew at the time commented on how "pleasantly surprised" advisers were that Indigenous people were able to carry out these organizational tasks.[20]

Stan Fulham who was the manager of Kinew from 1974 until 1981 outlined objectives from his book, "In Search of a Future." These objectives were to provide homes for Indigenous people from all economic backgrounds. The group believed that Indigenous people, whether well-off or economically challenged, would face discrimination in the urban housing market. They believed that part of the solution to this discrimination would be to create an Indigenous-controlled housing organization.[21] Their plan was to purchase older homes that were structurally sound and to renovate them to appropriate living standards. If they could rent these out at cost, they thought they could make them affordable to low-income Indigenous families. By creating a relatively large portfolio of at least 250 properties, they believed they could spread administrative costs across the units and achieve economies of scale.[22]

A second objective was to obtain subsidies from government to offset rents or housing purchases. This was a time when Canada's housing policy was undergoing significant transformation.[23] Previously, the federal government's approach had been construction grants for large public housing developments. Policy was now shifting toward assisting non-profit community groups in acquiring properties through government loans.[24] This policy was later to evolve into directly subsidizing rents for tenants. Kinew hoped to gain access to these new provisions.

20 David Henderson, "A Report on the Kinew Housing Experiment: (Time Period: June to December 1970)," in *The Indian-Métis Urban Probe*, ed. The Indian-Métis Friendship Centre and the Institute of Urban Studies (Winnipeg: The Institute of Urban Studies, 1970), 3, 6, 8, 9.

21 Fulham, *In Search of a Future*.

22 Ibid.

23 Gregory F. L. Suttor, *Still Renovating: A History of Canadian Social Housing Policy* (Montreal: McGill-Queen's University Press, 2016).

24 Ibid.

A third objective was to create a rent-to-own program. Fulham calls this "a vital principle in the development of Kinew Housing."[25] Kinew believed that most of its tenants would be coming from very poor housing conditions and would have little knowledge or experience in maintaining a home. They wanted their tenants to gain significant assets and they believed there would be greater incentives for families to care for their properties if they had the possibility of owning their homes.[26]

A fourth objective for Kinew was to provide employment to Indigenous people. A significant number of jobs would be created in renovating and maintaining the organization's portfolio. Kinew also intended to train an Indigenous person in property and project management. Finally, Kinew planned to spread their homes across the city. The organization believed that Indigenous families would face racism from neighbours wherever they were located. Scattering their portfolio would be a way to minimize racist reactions. As Meadmore said, they wished to avoid "ghettoization" of their families, especially in low-income neighbourhoods. "We bought homes in St. James, St. Boniface, and River Heights. The only place we didn't buy homes was in the North End."[27]

Most of Kinew's objectives proved challenging. Marvin Lipman, who was a senior administrator at The Government of Canada's national housing agency Central Mortgage and Housing Corporation at the time (CMHC) (now called "Canada" Mortgage and Housing), states matter-of-factly that Kinew received funding from a newly created CMHC fund. Stan Fulham tells the story differently: "Only after much controversy and dispute did the Central Mortgage and Housing Corporation ... finally agree to provide capital loans for the purchase of ... homes."[28]

25 Fulham, *In Search of a Future*, 16.

26 Ibid.

27 Meadmore, interview, 2022.

28 Fulham, *In Search of a Future*, 16.

Kinew believed they needed influential allies to help them to achieve their objectives. In 1970, they approached Lloyd Axworthy for assistance. Axworthy had been a candidate for the federal Liberal Party in the 1968 election and had worked in the office of John Turner, who was then Minister of Justice. He was influential with the government of the time in developing social housing policy.[29] In anticipation of changes to the federal government's National Housing Act, the minister responsible for housing had set aside resources within CMHC for "innovative forms of low-cost housing for families and individuals."[30] Axworthy persuaded CMHC to use some of these resources to fund Kinew as a "demonstration project." All of Kinew's housing work was then to be considered "research" on appropriate ways to meet the housing needs of urban Indigenous people.[31]

CMHC provided a loan of $360,000 for the purchase of Kinew houses.[32] For each home purchased, Kinew was to take out a separate mortgage with the federal agency. Normally, such mortgages required a ten percent down payment. Neither Kinew nor their prospective residents had such funds. Axworthy persuaded CMHC to recognize the time and commitment of the Indigenous board members of Kinew as "sweat equity" in the purchase of the homes.[33]

While Kinew could now buy houses, it still needed office space, management staff, and tenant support programs. Kinew made a separate application to CMHC for operating funds.[34] Despite the absence of

29 Suttor, *Still Renovating.*
30 Lipman, "Historical Review of CMHC's Urban Native Housing Activity."
31 J. D. McNiven, "An Evaluation of Kinew Housing Incorporated," In *Kinew Housing Incorporated* (Winnipeg: The Institute of Urban Studies, 1971).
32 David Henderson, "A Paper on Kinew Housing Incorporated," in *The Citizen and Neighbourhood Renewal: A Collection of Working Papers on Planning with People in the Inner City*, ed. Lloyd Axworthy (Winnipeg: The Institute of Urban Studies, 1972) McNiven, "An Evaluation."
33 Meadmore, interview, 2012.
34 David Henderson, "A Second Report on the 'Kinew Housing Incorporated' Experiment: (Time Period: January 1971 to July 1971)," in *Kinew Housing Incorporated* (Winnipeg: The Institute of Urban Studies, 1973).

workspace and administrative staff, the group decided to go ahead with their housing vision. Marion Meadmore and Delia Opekokew began to buy properties. Opekokew had been chosen to train as Kinew's real estate agent. In the organization's first two months, Opekokew and Meadmore purchased four properties.

After three months, CMHC agreed to provide operating funds. The grant CMHC provided, however, was only for $19,000 of the $41,000 that Kinew had requested.[35] CMHC would fund office space, a manager, and a secretary. It was unwilling, though, to provide resources for management training or to assist Indigenous people in adapting to urban living.[36] With operating funds, Kinew now sought to hire a manager and staff. They received twenty-eight applications for the management position. Of the Indigenous people who applied, virtually none had sufficient experience for the complex role of project and property management. Among the Non-Indigenous applicants, most had worked for large property management firms and expected salaries that were far beyond what Kinew could afford. This confirmed the organization's perception that management training ought to be a critical part of their program.

Rather than hire a non-Indigenous person as manager, Kinew asked two board members to step down and co-manage housing operations. Marion Meadmore and Marvin Hunt co-managed Kinew for the next three years. Marion and Opekekew purchased another sixty-two properties over the next eighteen months.[37] With the news that Kinew had received funding, Indigenous groups in Edmonton and the Lakehead region began to copy Kinew's formula.[38] Kinew's directors were asked to mentor Canative Housing in Alberta and a similar group

35 McNiven, "An Evaluation."

36 Ibid.

37 Henderson, "A Second Report."

38 David Henderson, "A Second Report on the 'Kinew Housing Incorporated' Experiment: (Time Period: January 1971 to July 1971)," in *Kinew Housing Incorporated* (Winnipeg: The Institute of Urban Studies, 1973).

in Brandon, Manitoba. In 1976, Kinew organized the Native Urban Housing Association of Canada (NUHAC), which advised the federal government and CMHC on policies to address urban Indigenous housing issues.[39]

Kinew became so competent at real estate transactions that when the IMFC decided to buy the Winnipeg Badminton Club, Kinew provided all the technical advice on the purchase. The new sports and recreation centre was renamed the Winnipeg Native Club.[40] In addition to being a centre for recreational uses, the building became a facility for Kinew's training work. Meadmore says, "We organized classes for all our tenants. We taught them how to drive cars, how to renovate, take all their plumbing apart and fix it themselves, and how to paint. We had classes every week."[41] To make it easier for tenants to attend classes, Kinew provided child care: "We set up...The Little Ones Nursery. We went and picked [the tenants] up by taxi...we would give their kids a good time in the nursery school, and they'd attend these classes."[42]

By mid 1973, Meadmore and Opekokew had served as real estate agents for two years and had handled all Kinew's transactions. At this point they decided to take some university courses. After having taken pre-law classes in Saskatoon, they each enrolled in law schools, Meadmore at the University of Manitoba and Opekokew at Osgoode Hall at York University in Toronto. Meadmore went on to found an all-female law firm in Winnipeg. Among her many honours, she was awarded the Order of Canada in 1985 for her contributions to the Indigenous community.[43] Opekokew became the first Indigenous lawyer to be called to the bar in Ontario and Saskatchewan. In 1995,

39 Fulham, *In Search of a Future*; Walker, "The Historical Development."
40 Hall, "The Early History"; McNiven, "An Evaluation."
41 Meadmore, interview, 2012.
42 Ibid.
43 Governor General, 2022; https://www.gg.ca/en/honours/recipients/146-13715.

she represented the family and the estate of Anthony O'Brien "Dudley" George, an activist who was shot by police at Ipperwash in Ontario.[44] Opekokew became an adjudicator with the Indian Residential Schools Adjudication Process, setting dollar amounts for harm done by residential schools. She authored several landmark publications on First Nations government and the Canadian Constitution.[45] Opekokew was the first woman to run for Grand Chief of the Assembly of First Nations.[46]

With the departure of Meadmore and Opekokew, Kinew had to search once again for a program manager. Meadmore says, "When I was getting ready to leave, we made sure that we got a good person in there to run [Kinew]. And he was. It turns out he really was. We really lucked-in there because Stan [Fulham] was... a wonderful manager. And he really made Kinew Housing go."[47] Stan Fulham had previously been executive director of the Manitoba Métis Federation (MMF).[48] In 1974, Fulham joined Kinew as general manager. Under his leadership, the organization's portfolio grew to 140 properties.[49] Fulham sought to implement more of Kinew's objectives, and in 1976, they were able to secure rent subsidies under the National Housing Act.[50] For social assistance recipients, the amount by which their rents exceeded their housing allowances on welfare was now to be covered by the federal and

44 Donna Sound and Tom Yun, "Lawyer and Residential School Survivor Delia Opekokew Fights for Justice, Reflects on Her Journey," *CTV News*, August 1, 2021, https://www.ctvnews.ca/canada/lawyer-and-residential-school-survivor-delia-opekokew-fights-for-justice-reflects-on-her-journey-1.5531607.

45 Delia Opekokew, *The First Nations: Indian Government and the Canadian Confederation* (Saskatoon: Federation of Saskatchewan Indians, 1980); Delia Opekokew, *The First Nations: Indian Government in the Community of Man* (Saskatoon: Federation of Saskatchewan Indians, 1982).

46 Sound and Yun, "Lawyer and Residential School Survivor."

47 Meadmore, interview, 2012.

48 Lawrence Barkwell, *History of the Manitoba Métis Federation and Memorable Métis Personalities of Manitoba* (Winnipeg: Louis Riel Institute, 2018). https://www.academia.edu/39137055/The_People_of_the_Metis_Nation_Q_Z.

49 Fulham, *In Search of a Future.*

50 Ibid.

provincial governments. Kinew's good quality housing was now affordable to people on assistance. The rents Kinew charged covered not only the organization's mortgage costs but also their administration expenses.

For tenants who were not receiving welfare benefits the subsidy system required them to pay twenty-five percent of their gross earnings (rent geared to income). Unfortunately, there was no maximum on how high these subsidized rents could rise. If people did well in employment, they sometimes found that the twenty-five-percent formula made Kinew Housing more expensive than housing in the unsubsidized market. Soon after the subsidy program began, a number of Kinew families left the organization to find cheaper units in the regular housing market. Kinew argued that this structure was a disincentive for families to leave welfare and find employment.[51]

Kinew ran into problems with CMHC over its rent-to-own program. Fulham says that when Kinew began, there was a verbal agreement with CMHC that a tenant could eventually take over their mortgage and own their home. In 1978, when Kinew tried to implement this, CMHC objected:

> CMHC refused and denied that it was party to such an agreement, although several reliable persons confirmed the agreement. CMHC officials demanded both the minutes of the meeting and the agreement. Since none could be produced, Native people were once again caught up in their own shortcoming, trusting in verbal agreements.[52]

CMHC finally agreed to allow tenants to take over their mortgages. However, CMHC expected the families to take over the mortgages at the current (1978) prices. Fulham says the values of the homes had doubled since they were originally purchased almost a decade earlier. Purchasing the homes at 1978 prices put mortgage payments well beyond what most Indigenous families could afford. The rent-to-own program, therefore, was never extensively implemented.

51 Ibid.

52 Ibid, 17–18.

Kinew also faced many challenges in attempting to hire Indigenous renovators. Initially, the organization wanted to award contracts to its own renovation crews at prices mutually agreed to with CMHC. The terms of their renovation funding, however, stipulated that contracts must be awarded through a competitive bidding process. In an effort to accommodate these terms, Kinew collaborated with the MMF in helping to manage Amisk ("Beaver") Enterprises. This was a for-profit company developed by the MMF to create employment for Indigenous workers. Kinew encouraged Amisk to bid on its renovation work. Amisk, however, faced the challenge of trying to combine significant levels of training in its program with the demands of competitive commercial production. Most of the publicly available training programs that it accessed were relatively short-term and did not fully equip the company's workforce for commercial productivity.

Amisk survived from 1974 to 1979. At its peak, the company had a workforce of thirty-five individuals. However, insufficient subsidies and lack of full training resources meant that, ultimately, the program had to shut down.[53] In 1981, Fulham described Kinew's successes. He listed them as:

a) Housing low income and multi-problem Indigenous families who were "not wanted in public housing programs or by private landlords."
b) Rehabilitating core area homes which, in some cases, would have been demolished.
c) Training and employing Native people in the repair and renovation of Kinew homes.
d) Assisting Indigenous families to integrate into urban communities.
e) Providing rental subsidies to families who needed such assistance.[54]

53 Ibid.

54 Ibid.

In 1981, Fulham retired and Lawrence Poirier became Kinew's new manager. Lawrence had been the organization's maintenance manager. Under his direction Kinew grew to 430 properties. Thirty of those homes were newly constructed by Kinew around the year 2006. In 2020, Kinew celebrated its fiftieth anniversary. Poirier says, "I think it was a milestone. When Kinew first started in 1970, I don't think [many] people [thought] it would last... In fact, in some documents... it was referred to us as the 'Kinew experiment.'"[55] Kinew is now involved in mentoring other Indigenous housing programs.

As Kinew was becoming established, a new wave of Indigenous activists began to address a different set of concerns in Winnipeg. These issues included the disastrous impacts of child welfare on Indigenous families, the need for culturally-based schools in neighbourhoods where the majority of children were Indigenous, and problems of poverty and low employment in Indigenous communities. Some of these activists were inspired by the work of organizers from the previous decade. As Ivy Chaske says,

> You know... the first group of women... like Mary Guilbault and Marion Meadmore... when I was growing up... I remember being proud when Marion became a lawyer, as if I knew her personally. And... when they'd accomplish things, you felt like you were part of it because they were in your lives, and whatever they did [you had] a sense of pride in the work that they did.[56]

In the early 1980s, there was a growing awareness that child welfare had impacted reserve communities with devastating effect. The details of the Sixties Scoop were being brought to light. (This is discussed in more detail in Chapter 7.) In a public inquiry, Associate Chief Justice Edmund Kimelman showed that twenty-five percent of Indigenous children apprehended in Manitoba were being placed

55 Lawrence Poirier, interview by Lawrence Deane and Kathy Mallett, 27 April 2021.

56 Chaske, interview, 2012.

outside the province, and many were being adopted outside the country.[57] After a review of all Indigenous child welfare files from 1981, the Manitoba Review Committee on the Indian and Métis Adoptions and Placements Chair Judge Kimelman stated "unequivocally" that "cultural genocide has been taking place in a systematic, routine manner."[58]

While the focus of this inquiry was on child welfare practices on reserve, Indigenous activists in urban areas such as Kathy Mallett, Louise Champagne, Linda Clarkson, and Ivy Chaske began to challenge child welfare practices in the city. They formed the Urban Native Child Welfare Coalition.[59] The same activists formed the implementation committee for Payuk Inter-Tribal (Housing) Co-op. This experience of challenging child welfare practices was important background for the principles and philosophy of Payuk.

Payuk (meaning "One" in Cree) was a project of the Métis Economic Development Training Program (MEDTP).[60] The MMF had created the MEDTP in 1983 (see Chapter 4 for further discussion). Louise Champagne was the manager of the program, and Russ Rothney was the training director. The training program created twenty-one committees in Métis communities across rural Manitoba, four of which were developed in Winnipeg. The committees were formed to generate ideas for economic development for their respective communities, and to choose individuals to be trained as Economic Development Officers

57 Manitoba Aboriginal Justice Inquiry, A.C. Hamilton, and C. M Sinclair, *Report of the Aboriginal Justice Inquiry of Manitoba,* Volume I; Chapter 14: Child Welfare (Manitoba: Province of Manitoba, 1991), http://www.ajic.mb.ca/volumel/chapter14.html.

58 Manitoba, *Children Need Families Not Courtrooms: Alternatives to Adversarial Litigation in Child Welfare,* A Special Report by the Office of the Children's Advocate, Manitoba, prepared by Dr. David Milward (Winnipeg: Office of the Children's Advocate, 2016), https://manitobaadvocate.ca/wp-content/uploads/MILWARD-FULL-web-1.pdf.

59 Manitoba Aboriginal Justice Inquiry, Hamilton, and Sinclair, *Report of the Aboriginal Justice Inquiry.*

60 MEDTP, Inc., *Currents of Change: Métis Economic Development* (Winnipeg: Pemmican Publications, 1986).

(EDOs). The EDOs would learn to assess the feasibility of projects and to implement them in their localities. The committees would then host the projects and provide community input. As Champagne says, "usually consultants do that work. And they walk away with that knowledge and it's not left in the community."[61]

In Winnipeg, the EDOs identified four projects: food security, child care, arts and crafts, and housing.[62] These projects eventually became Neechi Foods Co-op, the Niigaanaki Day Care Centre, and Payuk Inter-Tribal (Housing) Co-op. The arts and crafts program was folded into Neechi Foods. Payuk chose to form a co-op because this model created a sense of mutual ownership and sharing among its residents. These values were in line with Indigenous traditions of consensus decision-making and equitable distribution of resources. Co-op ownership was seen as a form of self-government in which Indigenous residents could make decisions about their own living situations.[63] Payuk's first purchase was a classic brown brick building on Qu'Appelle Avenue. Linda Keeper says, "We really loved that old building. They were beautiful old brownstones that were built in 1910."[64] Before Payuk could develop the building, however, the Winnipeg School Division decided it wanted the space as part of a playground for the new Sister Geraldine McNamara School. In 1988, the City of Winnipeg expropriated Payuk's new property. Keeper says, "That was a real blow to our dreams."[65] Russ Rothney says, "Huge work had gone into it [and now we] had to start all over again."[66]

61 Louise Champagne, interview by Lawrence Deane, 24 November 2021.

62 Russ Rothney, *Neechi Foods Co-op Limited: Lessons in Community Development* (Winnipeg: Neechi Foods Co-op, 1992).

63 Craig Hamilton, Tyler Hamilton, and Blair Hamilton, *In Search of Mino Bimaadiziwin: A Study of Urban Aboriginal Housing Cooperatives in Canada* (Winnipeg: SEED Winnipeg, Inc., and the Manitoba Research Alliance, 2014); Rothney, *Neechi Foods*.

64 Linda Keeper, interview by Lawrence Deane, 2 December 2021.

65 Ibid.

66 Rothney, interview.

Before demolition, the group salvaged whatever they could. According to Rothney, "We had a big sale. We sold bathroom fixtures and those clawed tubs ... oak boards off the floor."[67] Keeper adds, "I have pictures of Russ Rothney picking up the oak floorboards ... Ross apartments had a wrought iron gate ... it had 'Ross Apartments' in it ... We saved that and put 'Payuk' in it [instead]."[68] With the Qu'Appelle project ended, Payuk decided to construct their own building on Balmoral Street. Kathy Mallett remembers a meeting with the Co-op Development Branch and the architects:

> They were totally ignoring us ... and they're talking to the architects ... and I forget who spoke up ... We just said "Hey, look. We're the owners of the co-op—you talk to us ... Hello! We're not invisible!" But we were all women, right. ... [and] what do [women] know about housing?[69]

The pattern of stereotyping Indigenous people continued.

Payuk worked with the architects to design some special features in the building. To accommodate large families, they created additional three-bedroom units. Each of the three-bedroom units was to have two full bathrooms.[70] To build community, co-op members decided that everyone needed to help with chores around the building. At one important meeting, the members decided that there would be no alcohol. Champagne explains,

> Coming out of the child welfare coalition, we wanted a place that was safe for women. In this building there wasn't going to be any abuse or physical threats. Nor were any of the kids in this building ever going to get apprehended. Safe and secure housing for women. And if anyone was going to leave the house because they were disruptive, it wasn't going to be the women and children. That was the sort of commitment that was coming out of this group.[71]

67 Ibid.
68 Keeper, interview.
69 Kathy Mallett, interview by Lawrence Deane, 25 November 2021.
70 Keeper, interview.
71 Champagne, interview.

The seven-story, forty-two-apartment Payuk building was completed in 1989. Although largely successful, these housing projects also struggled in some ways to reach their objectives. In 1993, the federal government ended all support for the production of social housing.[72] This terminated the capital subsidies that Kinew was using to purchase homes.[73] Kinew has not purchased a home for renovation since 1993. When the original EDO at Payuk left the program, the co-op did not have the internal capacity to manage its operations. They engaged an outside, non-profit firm to handle their management.

Although these were disappointments, there were also considerable accomplishments. Kinew operates 430 well-maintained and affordable homes for Indigenous families, and the organization is currently mentoring four new Indigenous housing projects in Winnipeg.[74] In addition to housing at the Payuk building, Niigaanaki Day Care operates on the ground floor and provides accessible child care for parents who attend work or school. Keeper says, "It was a good thing to get something like [Payuk] built. Because you know, it benefited people. 'Till they could get on their feet, [or] go to school, [or] go to training."[75] Poirier says, "There [were] families that [brought] their problems with them. We can't solve all those problems. But at least we've given them a chance. Decent affordable housing gives people a chance to be stable, to set down some roots. We have families that have been with us thirty years. They've gone through bringing up their own kids, raising those children, and raising grandchildren."[76]

These achievements are the legacy of the early activists. Community organizers refused to tolerate mistreatment that surrounded urban migration. They were able to envision alternatives that reflected human respect, equity, and Indigenous values. Their programs have survived

72 Suttor, *Still Renovating*.

73 Poirier, interview.

74 Ibid.

75 Keeper, interview.

76 Poirier, interview.

for four decades. This is a tribute to the realism, the vision, the determination, and the wide-ranging skills of these early activists. Countless hours of unpaid time were invested to bring new programs into existence. The achievements of these leaders became an inspiration for succeeding generations and for other programs across the country.

After a lifetime of working for change, many of the interviewees for this project are still engaged in promoting social equity. Confronted by injustice, their responses continue to be the same as those of seventeen-year-old Marion Meadmore. When she came face to face with poverty in Winnipeg's inner city, she immediately concluded, "Somebody had to do something."

Bibliography

Barkwell, Lawrence. *History of the Manitoba Métis Federation and Memorable Métis Personalities of Manitoba.* Winnipeg: Louis Riel Institute, 2018.

Champagne, Louise. Interview by Lawrence Deane. 24 November 2021.

Chaske, Ivy. Interview by Darrell Chippeway, 2012. Recording at University of Manitoba Archives and Special Collections. Winnipeg, MB.

Hamilton, Craig, Tyler Hamilton, and Blair Hamilton. *In Search of Mino Bimaadiziwin: A Study of Urban Aboriginal Housing Cooperatives in Canada.* Winnipeg: SEED Winnipeg, Inc., and the Manitoba Research Alliance, 2014.

Fulham, Stanley A. *In Search of a Future.* Winnipeg: Kinew, 1981.

Governor General of Canada, 2022. https://www.gg.ca/en/honours/recipients/146-13715.

Hall, Leslie. "The Early History of the Winnipeg Indian Métis Friendship Centre, 1951–1968." In *Prairie Metropolis: New Essays on Winnipeg Social History,* edited by Esyllt W. Jones and Gerald Friesen. Winnipeg: University of Manitoba Press, 2000.

Henderson, David. "A Report on the Kinew Housing Experiment: (Time Period: June to December 1970)." In *The Indian-Métis Urban Probe,* edited by The Indian-Métis Friendship Centre and the Institute of Urban Studies. Winnipeg: The Institute of Urban Studies, 1970.

Henderson, David. "A Paper on Kinew Housing Incorporated." In *The Citizen and Neighbourhood Renewal: A Collection of Working Papers on Planning with People in the Inner City, The Future City No.3,* edited by Lloyd Axworthy. Winnipeg: The Institute of Urban Studies, 1972.

Henderson, David. "A Second Report on the 'Kinew Housing Incorporated' Experiment: (Time Period: January 1971 to July 1971)." In *Kinew Housing Incorporated.* Winnipeg: The Institute of Urban Studies, 1973.

Keeper, Linda. Interview by Lawrence Deane, 2 December 2021.

Lipman, Marvin. "Historical Review of CMHC's Urban Native Housing Activity." In *Urban Native Housing in Canada, Research and Working Paper No. 19,* by Marvin Lipman and Clare Brandt, 1986. Winnipeg: Institute of Urban Studies, University of Winnipeg.

Mallett, Kathy. Interview by Lawrence Deane, 25 November 2021.

Manitoba Aboriginal Justice Inquiry, A.C. Hamilton, and C. M Sinclair. *Report of the Aboriginal Justice Inquiry of Manitoba.* Volume I; Chapter 14: Child Welfare. Manitoba: Province of Manitoba, 1991. http://www.ajic.mb.ca/volumel/chapter14.html.

McCaskill, Don N. "Migration, Adjustment, and Integration of the Indian into the Urban Environment." Master's Thesis, Carlton University, 1970.

McNiven, J. D. "An Evaluation of Kinew Housing Incorporated." In *Kinew Housing Incorporated.* Winnipeg: The Institute of Urban Studies, 1971.

Meadmore, Marion. Interview by Darrell Chippeway, 19 April 2012. Recording at University of Manitoba Archives and Special Collections. Winnipeg, MB.

Meadmore, Marion. Interview by Lawrence Deane, 23 February 2022.

MEDTP, Inc. *Currents of Change: Métis Economic Development.* Winnipeg: Pemmican Publications, 1986.

MIB. *Urban Housing Survey.* Winnipeg: Manitoba Indian Brotherhood, 1971.

Milward, David. "Children Need Families Not Courtrooms: Alternatives to Adversarial Litigation in Child Welfare." *A Special Report by the Office of the Children's Advocate, Manitoba.* Winnipeg: Office of the Children's Advocate, 2016. https://manitobaadvocate.ca/wp-content/uploads/MILWARD-FULL-web-1.pdf.

Opekokew, Delia. *The First Nations: Indian Government and the Canadian Confederation.* Saskatoon: Federation of Saskatchewan Indians, 1980.

Opekokew, Delia. *The First Nations: Indian Government in the Community of Man.* Saskatoon: Federation of Saskatchewan Indians, 1982.

Peters, Evelyn J. "Developing Federal Policy for First Nations People in Urban Areas: 1945–1975." *Canadian Journal of Native Studies* XXI, 1 (2001): 57–96.

Poirier, Lawrence. Interview by Lawrence Deane and Kathy Mallett, 27 April 2021.

Rothney, Russ. Interview by Lawrence Deane, 24 November 2021.

Rothney, Russ. *Neechi Foods Co-op Limited: Lessons in Community Development.* Winnipeg: Neechi Foods Co-op, 1992.

Suttor, Gregory F. L. *Still Renovating: A History of Canadian Social Housing Policy.* Montreal: McGill-Queen's University Press, 2016.

Sound, Donna, and Tom Yun. "Lawyer and Residential School Survivor Delia Opekokew Fights for Justice, Reflects on Her Journey." *CTV News,* August 1, 2021. https://www.ctvnews.ca/canada/lawyer-and-residential-school-survivor-delia-opekokew-fights-for-justice-reflects-on-her-journey-1.5531607.

Walker, Ryan. "The Historical Development of the Canadian Urban Native Housing Program, from Winnipeg to Vancouver." In *Past Matters: Heritage in Planning History—Case Studies from the Pacific Rim,* edited by Caroline L. Miller and Michael Roche. Newcastle-upon-Tyne: Cambridge Scholars Publisher, 2007.

Chapter 4

Indigenous Economic Development in Winnipeg[1]

Lynne Fernandez and John Loxley

There is a rich history of Indigenous economic development in Winnipeg. This chapter traces the history of two examples of this development—the Neechi approach and the Neeginan approach—and highlights what made them unique to Winnipeg.

The term economic development is broadly used by economists to refer to policies and practices that improve social and economic life. Such actions can be targeted locally, regionally, nationally, or internationally. It can refer to how government programs can help lesser-developed, or third-world countries (meaning countries with low rates of industrialization, education, employment, access to healthcare, and with high rates of poverty) grow and join the ranks of fully developed, first-world economies such as ours. But despite

1 John Loxley was in the process of writing this chapter at the time of his death in July 2020. Co-editor Shauna MacKinnon further developed the material by drawing on Indigenous Archives Project interviews, as well as Dr. Loxley's previous work, in particular chapter 7, "Aboriginal Economic Development in Winnipeg," in Loxley's *Aboriginal, Northern, And Community Economic Development: Papers and Retrospectives* (Winnipeg: ARP Books, 2010). Lynne Fernandez further shaped the chapter, bringing it to this final version.

being a first-world country, Canada has pockets of extreme poverty, unemployment, and poor living conditions, including in First Nation communities and within large cities. The presence of these third-world conditions in a first-world country means that development theory from other parts of the world can be modified and applied to communities in Canada. As we will see, a development theory originally from the Caribbean was modified by members of Winnipeg's Indigenous community and put into action at a local level.

When economic development is focused on one community, it is referred to as Community Economic Development (CED). CED has a variety of approaches depending on which aspects of the local economy is deemed most important. It is common for government to be involved in CED approaches, and some would say government support is necessary for success, especially when working with marginalized communities.

When considering how any economic development strategy will work, it is necessary to consider how different sectors within the economy influence each other. For example, developing social services like job training is important for creating jobs, but only if there are job openings waiting for graduates. Furthermore, other questions arise such as whether we should be training job seekers for minimum wage positions with no job security or benefits.[2] What if parents don't have access to affordable child care? Who will oversee and provide child care—the private sector, government, or communities? Are child care workers paid a living wage so they can support their families?

Measuring economic improvement can be done in many ways. Someone in the business sector might only care about increasing profit and productivity to increase the wealth of those who own the business, productivity being measured by the number of resources—including workers and capital investment—required to produce a particular

2 Shauna MacKinnon, *Decolonizing Employment: Aboriginal Inclusion in Canada's Labour Market* (Winnipeg: University of Manitoba Press, 2015).

product or service. For example, fewer workers mean higher productivity. Many economists, politicians and businesspeople tend to focus on how much Gross Domestic Product (GDP)—the total dollar value of all economic activity for one year—grows or shrinks. Others may want to know whether income and wealth have been distributed more evenly. Do more people have jobs? What kind of jobs? Why is women's work unpaid? Has homelessness been reduced, access to education and healthcare improved? Economists debate these issues, come up with development theories, and often those theories influence government policy and groups involved in community development. Economists are not, and should not be, the only ones who ask these questions, and members of Winnipeg's Indigenous community indeed considered them when designing the approaches we examine here.

The issues raised above may seem unconnected, but they affect each other in complex ways. Economic development involves identifying and understanding the connections and taking action to make the parts of the economy complement each other and work as efficiently as possible. When Indigenous people design and implement a program or strategy to benefit their community, they are practicing Indigenous economic development.

Winnipeg's Indigenous community is not homogeneous, and not every approach Indigenous people take will be the same. Members of the community have different opinions, political views, and values. Those differences are evident in the history of Indigenous economic development in Winnipeg. Interviews with Indigenous leaders involved in this work touch on these differences, as well as the power struggles between Indigenous institutions, and some of the different ways in which economic development ideas have evolved over the decades.

Two Economic Development Initiatives

In this chapter, we examine two local initiatives: the Neechi approach, which was a version of CED based on principles designed by members of the Indigenous community, and which were derived from a theory of economic development called convergence theory; and the Neeginan approach, which was modified from its original plan which was to become a business-focused incubator model of development. This chapter covers the period between the 1950s and 2000. It starts with the story of Indigenous exclusion from the local economy, and then it explains how community leaders forged their own development paths to bypass the systemic racism that held the community back.

Racism and the long legacy of colonization have created difficult conditions for Winnipeg's urban Indigenous population, which faced—and face—higher than average rates of unemployment and poverty.[3] In response to this situation, Indigenous leaders created Indigenous-owned and Indigenous-run institutions to train and employ Indigenous people while building a network of businesses and social service providers to support the Indigenous community. Often supported by government, this network grew and changed over the decades, along with the Indigenous population.

This chapter does not cover all aspects of the network, nor does it discuss all the people who worked to improve conditions for the city's Indigenous people. Some of the people involved concentrated on employment equity, for example, so Indigenous people could get decent jobs in government and the private sector.[4] Others focused their attention on building Indigenous-owned private businesses that provided employment and training services. Greater detail about these and other efforts can be found in development economist John Loxley's 2010 book *Aboriginal, Northern, and Community Economic Development:: Papers and Retrospectives.*[5]

3 Loxley, *Aboriginal, Northern, and Community Economic Development*, 152, 159.

4 The Employment Equity Act of 1986 requires employers to limit criteria for employment to ability and qualifications. The intent is to remove barriers to employment experienced by persons with disabilities, women, visible minorities, and Aboriginal peoples.

5 Loxley, *Aboriginal, Northern, and Community Economic Development.*

Indigenous People in Winnipeg

The first reliable study of the Indigenous population in Manitoba was carried out in 1958. It was estimated that the Indigenous population represented just over one percent of Winnipeg's population.[6] The number of Indigenous people living in Winnipeg continued to grow quickly as Indigenous people moved to Winnipeg to seek opportunities. While Indigenous people migrated to the city for many reasons, the majority came seeking employment (eighty percent of women and fifty-five percent of men).[7] Economic development quickly became a priority for Indigenous activists throughout the 1960s and 1970s. One of those leaders, George Munroe, explains why he came to Winnipeg: "I came here because there was really nothing in my hometown ... I had ambitions ... there was something more than be a, a farm labourer or a bushman or a fisherman. These jobs didn't really appeal to me in the long-term, so I decided I'd come to the big city."[8]

For many like Munroe who went on to play a leadership role in Indigenous economic and social development, the 1960s and 1970s were periods of "consciousness raising." They describe Winnipeg as the centre of the Red Power political movement in Canada.[9] Indigenous youth in Winnipeg aligned closely with the US-based American Indian movement. It was a time when Indigenous people were becoming increasingly aware that social and economic inequity, including Indigenous poverty, homelessness, and unemployment, were intricately connected with colonization and systemic racism. According to Munroe,

> The big problem we had originally when I came into the city was there was a lot of racism, I mean it was really, really bad. And so that, that

6 Loxley, *Aboriginal, Northern, and Community Economic Development*, 152.

7 Lagassé cited in ibid.

8 George Munroe, Interview by Darrell Chippeway September 17, 2013. Recording at University of Manitoba Archives and Special Collections. Winnipeg, MB.

9 Ibid.

> was one of the issues that we were looking at. We were also looking at the fact that we didn't have a voice, right, either provincially or nationally, and so organization was one of the things that we were looking at. We were looking at poverty, homelessness, economic development, employment, education. I mean there were a whole, a slew of issues that kind of fell in our lap.[10]

This growing awareness inspired Indigenous youth to assume leadership of institutions such as the Indian and Métis Friendship Centre (IMFC), commonly called the Friendship Centre. This organization had originally been established to provide social services to Indigenous people coming to the city (see Chapter 2). The new generation of leaders sought to expand their role to include economic development, but progress was slow.[11]

The Incubator Approach and the Neeginan (Our Place) Vision

In the late 1960s, the Friendship Centre leadership began thinking about how it could bring the various Indigenous groups together to develop an Indigenous social and economic hub in Winnipeg. The centre developed this vision between 1972 and 1975 through its Neeginan (Cree for "Our Place") plan. Munroe, who was executive director of the Friendship Centre between 1972 and 1974, describes the early thinking behind Neeginan:

> We developed the concept because there were so many different little scatterings of groups. We all had to deal with the city, the province, the federal government and all the different departments. We said, why don't we just put everything in one place, right? Have one building. It will be kind of like a multipurpose facility, it will also be a cultural centre where we could bring all these organizations under one roof so that when people needed support or help, they wouldn't have to

10 Munroe, interview.

11 Ibid.

> run around all over hell's half acre, right? All the services would be in one place.[12]

The Neeginan vision included the creation of an Indigenous-run organization that operated its own housing, social service and economic facilities, and a detailed proposal was developed. According to Munroe, the proposal had considerable support from grassroots groups, but there was resistance among some other Indigenous organizations:

> You see, you got to remember they were always looking at the Friendship Centre as trying to gain more power...They weren't looking at what this was going to do for the community...what we were trying to do...They opposed it and fought against it and ultimately, they killed it.[13]

The Indian and Métis Friendship Centre was unable to put together the financial resources and coalition of Indigenous organization needed to realize the Neeginan plan. But others kept the vision alive. In 1981, Stan Fulham, former executive director of the Manitoba Métis Federation (MMF) and manager of Kinew Housing, proposed an adapted version of Neeginan. His experience with these organizations led him to conclude that if a combination of businesses, social services, and political organizations could share rent, financial services and even customers, they could help each other grow and thrive.[14] He had the idea to create the Native Economic Development and Employment Council (NEDECO), which would consist of representatives of Indigenous organizations and senior levels of government. The council would oversee the development of several initiatives with the aim to, in Fulham's words, "establish and promote a private business sector for Native People."[15] Fulham's approach was a more conserva-

12 Ibid.
13 Ibid.
14 Loxley, *Aboriginal, Northern, and Community Economic Development*, 194.
15 Fulham cited in ibid, 165.

tive version of the original IMFC proposal, emphasizing the private sector over government support.[16] While nothing came of this as the time, a version of the Neeganin Centre vision and Fulham's approach took hold in the Aboriginal Centre.

Neeginan Revisited: The Aboriginal Centre of Winnipeg

The socio-economic status of Indigenous people remained dire into the 1980s. Unemployment was more than five times higher than for non-Indigenous people, and those who were employed were more likely to have irregular employment.[17] Household incomes were found to be half of the average urban household, and most Indigenous families were dependent on government transfers, most commonly social assistance. Indigenous families were four times more likely than others to suffer a combination of shelter poverty, poor housing, and overcrowding.[18] Indigenous activists were determined to take control and return to the Neeginan idea.

Modification of the ideas initially articulated in the IMFC Neeginan plan re-emerged in in the late 1980s and early 1990s. The original Neeginan idea of bringing Indigenous organizations together under one roof was central to the proposal to establish the Aboriginal Centre in what used to be the Canadian Pacific Railway (CPR, formerly CP Rail) station located at Higgins Avenue and Main Street in Winnipeg's core. By 1992, the number of Indigenous organizations in Winnipeg had reached a critical mass, and a variety of economic opportunities presented themselves to those interested in building independence and capacity to self-manage. In particular, each organization was paying rent for space to non-Indigenous landlords. As Wayne Helgason, then the executive director of Ma Mawi Wi Chi Itata family resource centre points out, "Nobody owned anything, so the Aboriginal community

16 Ibid.
17 Ibid, 154.
18 Ibid.

had no stake in their buildings."[19] A light bulb turned on for Helgason when Ma Mawi Wi Chi Itata's landlord called him about a rent payment, explaining that the docking fees for his yacht in Kenora were due. At the time, Ma Mawi Wi Chi Itata was paying $144,000 a year in rent. Outraged, Helgason called local Indigenous activists and leaders, including Louise Champagne and Sandy Funk, to a meeting where it was recognized that Indigenous organizations needed to look at rent from an economic point of view. A follow-up meeting brought together Indigenous organizations that were paying a total of $500,000 annually in rent. Montrose Financial, a local mortgage and banking company, advised them that if they could reroute the rent payments to service a mortgage, they could borrow up to $4 million and purchase their own building.

This logic gave rise to a proposal to establish the Winnipeg Aboriginal Centre by buying the historic CPR station. The building, which had been built in 1905, was large—4 acres—and were it not for the Aboriginal Centre proposal, it might have ended up as a casino, an outcome that Helgason describes as "the worst kind of economic development."[20] Helgason, along with long-time Indigenous community activist Vern Morrissette and Patrick Falconer—a program manager working with the Winnipeg Core Area Initiative (CAI)—joined forces to figure out how to purchase the property.[21] They drew up a proposal, and twelve organizations committed to cooperate, with Ma Mawi Wi Chi Itata Centre as the anchor tenant. Five groups each put in $10,000, borrowed from Me-Dian Credit Union, an Indigenous-owned and Indigenous-run credit union (discussed in more detail in the CED section, below), in an offer to purchase for $1.1 million. The

19 Wayne Helgason, Interview by Darrell Chippeway March 8, 2013. Recording at University of Manitoba Archives and Special Collections. Winnipeg, MB.
20 Ibid.
21 The CAI was a $196 million, tripartite agreement (three levels of government) to aggressively attack Winnipeg's ongoing inner-city problems. The two phases of the CAI spanned a decade, from 1981 to 1991.

balance of the purchase price, together with the cost to repair this historical site, was cobbled together with help from all three levels of government, Canadian Pacific Railway (CPR), which reluctantly agreed to take back a mortgage, and later by means of loans provided by Assiniboine Credit Union.[22]

Helgason, Morissette, and Falconer next engaged in a process of political lobbying that won them the support of the federal, provincial, and municipal governments. Conservative Member of Parliament (MP) Dorothy Dobbie helped the group obtain $500,000 from the Historic Sites and Monuments Board of Canada. As a National Historic Site, the centre qualified for special funding for restoration and maintenance from the federal government, but provincial, municipal and other forms of funding were pursued too. The province and the city each contributed $200,000. The project developers credited specific government officials (Harvey Bostrom, executive director of the province's Northern Affairs Directorate, and Rick Frost, Chief Commissioner of the City of Winnipeg) for their support for the proposal. In addition, a charitable organization was established to accept public donations needed to leverage government grants for the repair and maintenance of the building.

Organizations began to move into the centre in November 1992, and the prospect of fulfilling Stan Fulham's hope for a centre that would incubate Indigenous businesses looked promising. But the building presented the tenants with many challenges. The CPR station had been allowed to deteriorate significantly in the years leading up to the sale. In the mid-1990s, Ma Mawi Wi Chi Itata decided to relocate for a variety of reasons, including the presence of asbestos in the building. The loss of its largest tenant created financial challenges for the Aboriginal Centre for many years.

Fortunately, under the leadership of Marileen Bartlett, the Centre for Aboriginal Human Resource Development (CAHRD), another major tenant of the Aboriginal Centre, responded to the asbestos

22 Loxley, *Aboriginal, Northern, and Community Economic Development*, 166.

concerns by developing a training course for Indigenous youth in asbestos removal. The trainees removed the asbestos in the Aboriginal Centre and several of them moved into permanent jobs doing the same work elsewhere. CAHRD recognized the connection between the need for a service (asbestos removal) and the opportunity for job training and employment created by that need. Taking action within the Aboriginal Centre not only improved the long-term viability of the physical building, but it also strengthened CAHRD's program offerings and improved labour market opportunities for local youth.

CAHRD has since evolved into an important institution for Indigenous training and employment and for helping Indigenous people.[23] Through the Aboriginal Centre, trainees are offered life-skills supports, literacy, child care, and housing. Still based in the Aboriginal Centre, CAHRD negotiates job access to well-paying mainstream occupations such as welding and aeronautical jobs and helps support trainees to qualify for them. Since 1992, the Aboriginal Centre has provided student housing to members of the Indigenous community. Fulham's hope that privately-run businesses and commercial interests would thrive has not been fully realized, but the centre remains committed to its goal of strengthening the Indigenous community's economic base in Winnipeg's core and helping Indigenous job seekers train for decent jobs in the trades.[24]

The Aboriginal Centre's first chief executive officer Bill Shead was guided by the philosophy, "It's not enough to dream. We must do!" Judged by this standard, the Aboriginal Centre has been a success. It brought a longstanding vision of Indigenous economic development to fruition—one that understood the need to connect local economic activity so different players could support each other. In 2000, Circle of Life Thunderbird House, the "spiritual anchor to the Neeginan

23 Bartlett negotiated an Aboriginal Human Resource Development Agreement (AHRDA) for urban training in 1995–97 and managed to negotiate a funding agreement with the three different levels of government.

24 Loxley, *Aboriginal, Northern, and Community Economic Development*, 194.

project," opened its doors.[25] Designed by renowned Indigenous architect Douglas Cardinal, this beautiful building, located across the street from the Aboriginal Centre, provides a meeting space for ceremonies, conferences, and feasts. Although Thunderbird House has had some struggles over the years, it remains an important Indigenous space.

Given that private enterprise is such a powerful force in the Canadian economy, Fulham's focus on developing Indigenous private business makes sense. But others in the Indigenous community wanted to take a different path. They wanted to develop economic opportunities more in keeping with their cultural roots.

Traditional Economies

Long-time Winnipeg Indigenous activist and economic planner Louise Champagne, a Winnipegger with a long history in both Indigenous activism and co-operative enterprises, makes a strong case for the economic effectiveness of traditional economies:

> I recognize that, historically, that sharing and caring culture at one time, before the introduction of commercial trade—before the fur trade—that that sharing and caring culture was based on an economy that was all about people involved in producing for the wellbeing of the community. Everybody was involved: women, children, men, women, and children were involved in producing for the wellbeing of the community. That was the kind of economy that existed here—they were healthy economies, even though we didn't have economists running around, writing down the GDP.[26]

The idea of a sharing and caring economy resonated with many in Winnipeg's Indigenous community. Community members wanted to develop a model for the "wellbeing of the community" that was controlled by the community and that could co-exist in a modern

25 Winnipeg Architecture Foundation, n.d. https://winnipegarchitecture.ca/715-main-street/.

26 Louise Champagne. Interview by Darrell Chippeway, 29 March 2013.

capitalist society more concerned with corporate profitability than healthy communities. Community Economic Development (CED) provided a theoretical framework to accommodate that model.

Community Economic Development (CED)

A CED approach to development includes "an economic analysis of the community and research and decision making aimed at drawing up a plan of action to create or maintain the kind of community that people have collectively determined to be desirable."[27] CED drives decisions around who has ownership of capital and natural resources; the choice of products, markets, and investments; the scale of production and kinds of technology used; and how to ensure everyone can participate in economic activity.[28] Versions of CED can include government support, like subsidies or procurement contracts. There is an understanding that such investment can result in a net gain when previously unemployed or underemployed people receive training and become employed in decent jobs. The cost of other social services decreases, health improves, and even costs associated with incarceration can be reduced.[29]

Winnipeg's Indigenous community put its own stamp on a strategy initially developed in the 1970s by local development economist John Loxley when he was senior policy advisor for the provincial government. The Northern Manitoba Development Strategy modified an international development theory and devised a "comprehensive economic and social development project" for parts of Manitoba's North.[30]

27 Lotz quoted in Loxley, *Aboriginal, Northern, and Community Economic Development*, 20.

28 Loxley, *Aboriginal, Northern, and Community Economic Development*, 21.

29 Kirsten Bernas and Blair Hamilton, *Creating Opportunities with Green Jobs: The Story of BUILD and BEEP* (Winnipeg: The Canadian Centre for Policy Alternatives-Manitoba, 2013), https://www.policyalternatives.ca/sites/default/files/uploads/publications/Manitoba%20Office/2013/01/Build%20Beep_0.pdf.

30 Loxley, *Aboriginal, Northern, and Community Economic Development*, 93–130.

What became known as the Great Northern Plan combined ideas developed by the Caribbean economist C.Y. Thomas and Canadian economist Harold Innis. Thomas's work with low-income communities in the Caribbean led him to develop what came to be called "a convergence strategy." This means a community produces what it needs and consumes what it produces, in contrast to a divergent economy that exports what it produces and imports what it consumes.[31] A convergence strategy stops the leakage of profits away from the community and has them working locally. In his study of how the Canadian economy relied too heavily on the export of raw materials—which he called "staples"—to the exclusion of developing a domestic manufacturing sector to process those raw materials, Innis identified the importance of what he called backward and forward linkages. Linkages are the connection between different sectors of the economy. For example, forests provide the raw material for processing into lumber (a forward linkage), which gets turned into housing (a final demand linkage). The timber may be transported by truck (a backward linkage). A convergence strategy would seek to produce a range of goods to develop as many backward, forward, and final-demand linkages as possible. Ideally, these products would have high growth potential to generate as many jobs as possible in, say, sawmills, construction, and transportation.[32]

The Great Northern Plan was never put into action, but the idea that the Indigenous community could take control of local resources and provide jobs and housing for First Nation communities was aligned with Champagne's vision of "producing for the wellbeing of the community."

31 Laura Lamb, "Towards an Economic Theory of Community Economic Development," in *Transforming or Reforming Capitalism: Towards a Theory of Community Economic Development*, ed. John Loxley (Winnipeg: Fernwood Publishing, 2007).

32 John Loxley, *The Economics of CED—A Report Prepared for the Native Economic Development Program* (Winnipeg: University of Manitoba, 1985), 51.

The Neechi Principles

It was in Winnipeg in the 1980s that Indigenous activists put the ideas developed in the Great Northern Pan into action. In the process, they developed what have come to be known as the Neechi Principles (Neechi means "friend" in Ojibway/Cree). These ten principles form an exhaustive and demanding set of criteria inspired by the vision of community economic development first articulated in the Great Northern Plan. In the early 1980s, there were two training sessions held for Métis and Indian economic development and finance officers who were familiar with the Great Northern Plan. They developed an economic development strategy that eventually evolved into the ten Neechi Principles still recognized today by Manitoba's CED sector:

1. Use locally produced goods and services.
2. Produce goods and services for local use.
3. Re-invest profits back into the local economy.
4. Create long-term employment of local residents.
5. Develop local skills.
6. Encourage local decision making.
7. Consider the physical and mental health of community residents.
8. Encourage development that makes neighbourhoods attractive and safe and protects the environment.
9. Improve neighbourhood stability through long-term residency and decent housing.
10. Spread human dignity for all.

An eleventh principle was added later:

11. Support other CED initiatives such as cooperatives and social enterprises.[33]

33 Sara Wray Enns, *Community Economic Development in Manitoba. Theory, History, Policy, and Practice* (Winnipeg: The Canadian Centre for Policy Alternatives-Manitoba, 2018), 5, https://www.policyalternatives.ca/sites/default/files/uploads/publications/Manitoba%20Office/2018/01/CED_in_MB_Theory_History_Policy_Practice.pdf.

The training sessions that spawned the Neechi Principles were sponsored by the Manitoba Métis Federation and the Assembly of Manitoba Chiefs (AMC) but run independently. The programs trained over fifty Indigenous economic development workers, most of whom were later employed by Indigenous organizations in Manitoba. Out of these courses, which combined rigorous classroom work with practical on-the-job experience, came a series of community planning meetings in the summer of 1985, run by the trainees. Four projects were identified in these meetings as being high on the list of priority needs in the community in Winnipeg: a food store, a housing co-op, a child care centre, and a crafts shop. The trainees proceeded to appraise each, working in conjunction with project working groups. All but the last of these was implemented in the form of Neechi Foods Co-op, the Niigaanaki Day Care Centre, and Payuk Inter-Tribal (Housing) Co-op, and in the early years they were loosely "federated" under the umbrella of the Winnipeg Native Family Economic Development (WNFED), a mutual support group. According to Louise Champagne, the group provided a means by which members could draw on each other's experience and knowledge and be paid for their efforts when the initiatives were start-ups and couldn't pay members:

> [WNFED] was incorporated as a development corporation and some of the people connected with that development corporation were able to land some other paid work because Neechi couldn't pay them or Payuk couldn't pay them, and they wanted to stay involved and so they were able to bid on other say research contracts and get some paid work going and stay connected with the project development work.[34]

Perhaps the most clearly articulated approach to using the Neechi Principles in Indigenous economic development was eventually put forward a decade later by members of the Neechi Foods Co-op.[35]

34 Ibid.48.
35 See Winnipeg Native Family Economic Development Inc. *It's Up to All of Us.*

Neechi Foods Co-op Ltd. (1991–2018) was a worker co-op that operated a grocery store and Indigenous specialty shop in the inner-city. The objectives of the co-op were to offer Indigenous people a better selection of food at better prices; to promote community health; to employ local Indigenous people and promote Indigenous pride; to keep money circulating in the community; to foster sharing, cooperation, and local control; and to create capital for new projects.

Following the Neechi Principles, Neechi Foods Co-op outlined ten community development criteria by which to assess proposed or actual community initiatives. The first three align with the "convergence" approach to economic strategy that Loxley proposed in the Great Northern Plan, meaning they promote goods and services that are produced in the local economy, and the reinvestment of profits locally. This means that income earned in the inner city should, as far as possible, be spent in the inner city, and preferably on goods and services which are produced there. This contrasts with the reality that inner-city income leaks away when it is spent elsewhere in the city on goods and services which are not produced in the inner city, referred to as the "leaky bucket" phenomenon. By implementing the Neechi Principles, Neechi Foods Co-op members and supporters encouraged inner-city residents and those earning income in the inner city to use their purchasing power to benefit the local community. This would reduce economic leakage and maximize economic linkages within the inner city, thereby reducing dependence on outside markets and building greater community self-reliance.

Neechi Foods Co-op trained and employed community members in accordance with the fourth principle to create long-term employment for inner-city residents. This helped reduce dependency on welfare and foodbanks. It also helped to build personal and community esteem, to increase the amount of personal income available to spend in the community, and to enable people to live more socially productive lives. Related to this, the fifth principle calls for the training of local residents in the practice of community development. The sixth principle or guideline is the encouragement of local decision making through local cooperative forms of ownership (including credit unions), control, and grassroots participation. The aim is to strengthen community self-determination as people work together to meet community needs.

Principles seven and eight recognize the importance of community development in promoting public health and a safe and attractive physical environment. The ninth principle stresses the centrality of, firstly, achieving greater neighbourhood stability by providing more dependable housing; secondly, encouraging long-term residency (complemented by the Payuk housing co-op discussed next); and lastly, creating a base for long-term community economic development.

Finally, the whole approach is premised on the safeguarding and enhancement of human dignity. While there is a personal dimension to this in the form of promoting self-respect, much of the emphasis is social: recognizing the need to generate community spirit, encourage gender equality, and respect seniors and children. The Neechi criteria also emphasize social dignity regardless of physical or mental differences, national or ethnic background, colour or creed. Above all, community development should promote Indigenous pride.

In 2013, Neechi Food Co-op relocated from its small space on Dufferin Avenue to Neechi Commons, a much larger, shared space on Main Street. Neechi Co-op experienced a number of challenges and in 2018 it halted its operations. Its twenty-seven-year span in the highly competitive grocery sector was no small accomplishment, and hopefully the community will be able to apply lessons learned from the experience to new opportunities.

The housing operation affiliated with WNFED is the Payuk Inter-Tribal Co-op, a 42-unit apartment block and five duplex units (see Chapter 3). Co-ops by nature lend themselves to the Neechi Principles by encouraging control by residents, rather than by a corporate entity that owns the assets. In keeping with the Neechi Principles concerning security and long-term residency, Payuk is dedicated to providing housing for Indigenous women and children in a supportive environment.

In contrast to a private, profit-driven model, rents are subsidized by the Manitoba government and tenants pay a rate based on their income.[36] The Niigaanaki (Nee Gawn Ah Kai) Day Care Centre is located in the Payuk building. It employs six people and has space for thirty children. Having a daycare located in the same complex makes it easier for residents to access child care and provides the local community with employment opportunities. Having control over the curriculum also allows the community to deliver culturally appropriate care and education.

Ma Mawi Wi Chi Itata Centre (see Chapter 7), was also associated with WNFED in its early days of development. The Winnipeg Coalition on Native Child Welfare which initiated the development of Ma Mawi Wi Chi Itata Centre worked closely with the Economic Development Training Program, underlining the holistic, integrated approach to economic and social reform subscribed to and advocated for by many in the Indigenous community, and as articulated in the Neechi Principles.

The Neechi approach has influenced the economic development planning of Indigenous groups in Winnipeg's inner city, including the Aboriginal Centre, which articulated an economic planning process that embraced the principles noted above.[37] The aforementioned Me-Dian Credit Union provides an example of how the Indigenous community took control of a crucial aspect of economic planning: providing financial resources.

Me-Dian Credit Union

In 1978, a group of Indigenous activists, including Bill Shead, saw the need for a financial institution to provide services to the Indigenous community. The Me-Dian (from Métis and In*dian*) Credit Union was the first full service Indigenous-owned financial institution in

36 Loxley, *Aboriginal, Northern, and Community Economic Development*, 173.
37 Ibid, 169.

Canada.[38] In a 2013 interview for the Indigenous Archives Project, Shead explains:

> [What] the Me-Dian Credit Union could do that was absolutely an essential first step... was to provide financial services to the Aboriginal community as a whole, because every Aboriginal person or every person working in today's society needs to be able to deposit money in a bank, to write cheques, to get a credit card, to have safety deposit boxes, and all these other financial services that banks and credit unions provide. The trouble is that most banks and credit unions twenty-five years ago were not Aboriginal-friendly. So with the Aboriginal community and the Me-Dian Credit Union we now have a place we can call home.
>
> We still go through the same discipline—do you have the credit worthiness to be able to get a loan... However, over time we were able to demonstrate to Credit Union Central and other people within the credit union movement that the Me-Dian Credit Union was providing an essential service to the Aboriginal community. And because we developed relationships with individuals, we were able to provide nice tailor-made financial services, to bands, to some businesses and we became the most profitable credit union of our size in Manitoba.[39]

With its main branch on Selkirk Avenue in Winnipeg, Me-Dian Credit Union is a co-op, owned by its members.[40] The co-op model lends itself to the Neechi principles of keeping money circulating in the community and of local decision making through local cooperative forms of ownership. Me-Dian offers financial services to individual and corporate members and facilitated the successful bid to purchase the Aboriginal Centre.

38 Me-Dian Credit Union, "About/History," accessed May 4, 2021, https://www.mediancu.mb.ca/history.

39 Bill Shead. Interview by Darrelly Chippeway, 14 March, 2013. Recording at the University of Manitoba Archives and Special Collections. Winnipeg, MB.

40 Me-Dian Credit Union, "About/History."

Different but the Same

Although they are different in terms of individual versus collective approaches, the Fulham/Neeginan approach and the Neechi approach are similar in that each recognize the importance of Indigenous involvement in the process; they both stress the importance of developing linkages and mutually supporting economic initiatives; they both recognize the importance of having support services available to Indigenous businesses, and especially of appropriate training; they both argue for the importance of providing decent long-term housing; and they both argue for the social desirability of non-Indigenous support for Indigenous ventures, even when more lucrative investment outlets or cheaper purchases could be had elsewhere.[41]

There are also differences between the two approaches. Firstly, the Neechi approach, much like the earlier IMFC Neeginan model, is much more clearly grounded in grassroots community activism than is the Fulham/Neeginan model and its variants, and it doesn't put as much emphasis on the role Indigenous political organizations play in the economic development process. Secondly, the Neechi model attaches a much greater importance to community ownership and control than did the Neeginan model developed by Fulham, who was mainly focused on promoting support for privately-owned Indigenous businesses. Similar to George Munroe's claim of broad community support for the IMFC Neeginan proposal, a survey of inner-city residents showed significant support for a community ownership model compared with private business ownership.[42]

Thirdly, the Neechi approach is a much more holistic one, in which economic development is seen as one aspect—albeit a very important one—of healthy communities, in which economic opportunity, health, educational development, and social and environmental stability go hand in hand. This is not to say that Fulham would have disagreed with the Neechi approach, he just didn't articulate a comprehensive, holistic

41 Loxley, *Aboriginal, Northern, and Community Economic Development*,169.
42 Ibid.

approach in the same way. Fourthly, Neechi attaches less importance to the physical aggregation of enterprises under one roof, preferring more spatial balance and securing supportive services and economies of scale in other ways. And finally, the Neechi approach promotes restoring economic balance and community self-reliance through economic restructuring, which challenges the logic of the market economy. Fulham's Neeginan approach, on the other hand, accepts the dominant market on its own terms and seeks to break into it with state assistance.

Sixty Years Later

According to Canada's 2016 census, Winnipeg's Indigenous population constituted twelve percent of the total population, up considerably from sixty years ago when it was just over one percent.[43] As this chapter has shown, Indigenous institutions have grown along with the population. When asked if things have improved in Winnipeg, Munroe responded,

> I mean no question about that, I mean economically, socially, politically. When we were organizing in Winnipeg back in the '70s, we had one university graduate. Well look around today. We've got doctors, lawyers, social workers, teachers ... We've infiltrated the provincial government and the federal government politically.[44]

His final observation was:

> I think there's a recognition there by a lot of people that, number one, we're here to stay and we're not going to go away anytime soon and

43 Thomas Anderson, "Results from the 2016 Census: Housing, Income and Residential Dissimilarity Among Indigenous People in Canadian Cities," *Insights on Canadian Society*, Statistics Canada, December 10, 2019, https://www150.statcan.gc.ca/n1/pub/75-006-x/2019001/article/00018-eng.htm; Loxley, *Aboriginal, Northern, and Community Economic Development*, 152.

44 George Munroe. Interview by Darrell Chippeway, 17 September, 2013. Recording at the University of Manitoba Archives and Special Collections. Winnipeg, MB.

we're going to continue coming, flooding the cities, so something has to happen.

The approaches highlighted here reflect the intelligence and tenacity of Winnipeg's first Indigenous activists. The positive changes Munroe notes—improved levels of education, decent jobs, political clout—will have at least partly emerged from the economic development efforts these activists undertook.

Bibliography

Anderson, Thomas. "Results from the 2016 Census: Housing, Income and Residential Dissimilarity Among Indigenous People in Canadian Cities." *Insights on Canadian Society*. Statistics Canada, December 10, 2019. https://www150.statcan.gc.ca/n1/pub/75-006-x/2019001/article/00018-eng.htm.

Bernas, Kirsten, and Blair Hamilton. *Creating Opportunities with Green Jobs: The Story of BUILD and BEEP.* Winnipeg: The Canadian Centre for Policy Alternatives-Manitoba, 2013. https://www.policyalternatives.ca/sites/default/files/uploads/publications/Manitoba%20Office/2013/01/Build%20Beep_0.pdf.

Lamb, Laura. "Towards an Economic Theory of Community Economic Development." In *Transforming or Reforming Capitalism: Towards a Theory of Community Economic Development*, edited by John Loxley. Winnipeg: Fernwood Publishing, 2007.

Loxley, John. *The Economics of CED—A Report Prepared for the Native Economic Development Program.* Winnipeg: University of Manitoba report, 1985.

Loxley, John. *Aboriginal, Northern, and Community Economic Development Papers and Retrospectives.* Winnipeg: ARP Books, 2010.

MacKinnon, Shauna. *Decolonizing Employment: Aboriginal Inclusion in Canada's Labour Market.* Winnipeg: University of Manitoba Press, 2015.

Me-Dian Credit Union. "About/History." Accessed May 4, 2021. https://www.mediancu.mb.ca/history.

Munroe, George. Interview by Darrell Chippeway September 17, 2013. Recording at University of Manitoba Archives and Special Collections, Winnipeg, MB.

Shead, Bill. Interview with Darrell Chippeway, March 14, 2013. Recording at the University of Manitoba Archives and Special Collections. Winnipeg, MB.

Winnipeg Architecture Foundation. www.https://winnipegarchitecture.ca/.

Winnipeg Native Family Economic Development Inc. *It's Up to All of Us: A Guide to Community Economic Development in Winnipeg's Inner-City*. February, 1993.

Wray Enns, Sara. *Community Economic Development in Manitoba. Theory, History, Policy, and Practice.* Winnipeg: The Canadian Centre for Policy Alternatives-Manitoba, 2018. https://www.policyalternatives.ca/sites/default/files/uploads/publications/Manitoba%20Office/2018/01/CED_in_MB_Theory_History_Policy_Practice.pdf.

Chapter 5

Indigenous Education and the Thunder Eagle Society:

The Fight for Aboriginal Schools[1]

Shauna MacKinnon and Kathy Mallett

> "We want a school of our own. We want a place where we can go to be with our own people and learn in our own way."[2]—Vern Morrissette

In 1991, the Winnipeg School Division's first and only Aboriginal High School opened its doors in the city's North End. The school is located on the corner of Stella Avenue and Salter Street, just north of the Slaw Rebchuk Bridge, which spans the Canadian Pacific Railway yards that separate the North End from the rest of the city. A few years later, Niji Mahkwa opened its doors on Flora Avenue, adjacent to Children of the Earth in the old Aberdeen High School building. Niji Mahkwa

1 The terms Aboriginal and Indigenous are used throughout this chapter. The term "Aboriginal" was commonly used during the period and is the term used in historical documents and interviews. The term "Indigenous," is more commonly used today. Both terms include First Nation, Métis, and Inuit peoples.

2 Vern Morrissette, interview by Larry Morrissette, February 8, 2013. Recording at the University of Manitoba Archives and Special Collections. Winnipeg, MB.

offers Indigenous curriculum to students in grades 1 through 8. Niji Mahkwa was the second phase of a community-led campaign to ensure that Indigenous children in Winnipeg had access to culturally relevant curriculum, Indigenous teachers, and a more positive educational experience. These two schools continue to operate in the North End of Winnipeg and are an important part of the story of Indigenous resistance and development in Winnipeg's inner city.

Community-led Activism Behind Children of the Earth and Niji Mahkwa Schools Leading to the Thunder Eagle Society

The Children of the Earth High School website provides this brief history of the school:

> In 1988 [following a strong, active, and sustained community activism], the Winnipeg School Division, in consultation and cooperation with various community groups such as the Thunder Eagle Society, Urban Aboriginal Educational Advisory Committee, and parent groups, began what was then considered a bold undertaking. They established a high school in Winnipeg's North End that emphasized Aboriginal culture, language, and academics. A school that harkens back to the lessons of our ancestors, and made valid the concept of Aboriginality in the education system. It allowed First Nations youth the freedom to practice their culture in a place where it was once prohibited, in schools. In 1991, it opened as the "Aboriginal High School" and after consultation with its educational community, the name "Children of the Earth" was submitted by a student and adopted.

The Winnipeg School Division Inner-City District describes Niji Mahkwa as "upholding the belief that all children have an inherent right to the highest quality of holistic education. The integration of traditional, cultural teachings in a supportive learning environment will provide students with strengths and skills to meet the challenges of life."[3]

3 Niji Mahkwa School. https://www.winnipegsd.ca/nijimahkwa/page/6570/our-visionWinnipeg School Division. Accessed January 28, 2023.

These official chronicles on the history and genesis of these schools gloss over the fact that Children of the Earth and Niji Mahkwa schools would not exist if not for the determination of Indigenous activists and the grassroots Thunder Eagle Society. Through this organization, community activists spearheaded the campaign for Indigenous schools in Winnipeg. Children of the Earth and Niji Mahkwa schools did not result from a school division-led process of community consultation. These two schools would not exist without the fight put up by the community, which was fuelled by their discontent and vision for a better educational system for the community and the next generation of youth. Vern Morrissette was one of the early activists and a founding member of the Thunder Eagle Society.[4] In a 2013 interview with his brother Larry Morrissette, also a founding member, Vern Morrissette reflects on the history of the schools. He describes Children of the Earth High School as an important story needing to be told from the perspective of those who fought hard for it. He explains, "They resisted us, they resisted us. They resisted...We lobbied them for two-three years. We forced them to listen to us. There were a couple of sensitive years...Who were these Indians making demands?" This chapter tells that story from the perspective of those involved in both community activism and the Thunder Eagle Society, as well as from the perspective of the Indigenous school trustees and bureaucrats who became allies and fought within the system to see the community vision come to life.

The Vision

The community effort that led to the development of Children of the Earth High School and later Niji Mahkwa school began with the vision of Indigenous activists and community youth workers Larry Morrissette and David Blacksmith. Their work sowed the seeds that led to the Thunder Eagle Society.

4 Vern Morrissette was interviewed by his brother Larry Morrissette in 2013. Larry, who Vern describes as a leader in the movement to establish an "Aboriginal Survival School" passed away in 2016.

Larry Morrissette and David Blacksmith were employed by Ma Mawi Wi Chi Itata Centre during the 1980s. Larry Morrissette was a team leader for the Youth Program and Blacksmith was a cultural youth worker for the program. Vern Morrissette describes Ma Mawi Wi Chi Itata Centre (see Chapter 7) as "the catalyst that started everything in the community" during that period.[5] Ma Mawi Wi Chi Itata Centre initially played a significant role in Children of the Earth High School by supporting Larry Morrissette and Blacksmith's work with youth, and later by encouraging them in their political advocacy for an Aboriginal school. They organized youth/elder workshops at the City of Winnipeg's Freight House on Isabel Street in the inner city. A central purpose of the workshops was to connect Indigenous youth with their Indigenous cultures and to give them an opportunity to sound their own voices and express their own vision for the future. Blacksmith, a charismatic man deeply rooted in culture, was particularly instrumental in getting youth motivated and animated to speak out. At one of those workshops, youth discussed the continuing challenges they experienced at school, challenges that Vern Morrissette describes as all too familiar in his interview with his brother Larry in 2013. He reminds Larry of the important role that he played in rallying the community:

> You [Larry] were one of the most significant people...You were the one who was working to percolate the young people back then with those elder/youth conferences that you used to put on at the Freight House.
>
> You were there helping to generate the energy and the strength and the confidence of the youth. And you were there helping them speak up about what they wanted.
>
> I remember how powerful they were. They were saying they were tired of going to schools and feeling racism and discrimination, all

5 Vern Morrissette, interview by Larry Morrissette, 8 February, 2013. Recording at University of Manitoba Archives and Special Collections. Winnipeg, MB.

> the stuff that I've gone through that they were still going through at the time, same bullshit...They were saying "we don't want that crap anymore"...One of the main things they said was: we want a school of our own. We want a place where we can go to be with our own people. And learn in our own way.
>
> They were tired of going to schools and feeling discrimination and racism.
>
> The same shit bullshit. We are tired and we want our own school.
>
> We were there...you were there, I was there, Wilfred Buck, David Blacksmith, all the women and the youth.
>
> We said, "that's it" and what we started to do is we organized and lobbied the school division. We went to their board meetings.

In fact, Larry Morrissette did more than simply engage and motivate the youth, as important as that was. He was the key organizer—the social broker—who recruited and connected community activists, teachers, politicians, and allies that were all required to bring this initiative to life. His brother Vern describes Larry as "the silent Okijjiida (warrior) who, with his gentle spirit and ability to connect people and their ideas, facilitated the organizing of people with the social conscious and the skill sets necessary to forward the vision into reality."

In October 1989, Larry and Vern Morrissette, David Blacksmith, Wilfred Buck, Connie West, Judy Dasilva, Chickadee Richard, Sharon Richard, Luke Arquette, and many others who supported the initiative acted as individuals and began to lobby the Winnipeg School Division No.1 to establish an Aboriginal school. To get the school division's attention, they staged a sit-in at the division's board office. They delivered a presentation in Cree to the board to make the point that Indigenous languages are critical to the education of Indigenous youth.

The Winnipeg School Division was initially resistant, if not hostile, to the concept of an Aboriginal school. Activists recall the division staff questioning who they represented and being unable to conceptualize a role for the community in the formal education system. Division staff recommended that the group work through the Urban Aboriginal Advisory Committee as the division's "official" source of advice on Aboriginal education. The Urban Aboriginal Advisory Committee was a formal structure sanctioned by the Winnipeg School Division. The committee was comprised of Aboriginal educators and select members of the community with cultural or professional "credentials." The committee was co-chaired by George Desnomie, the executive director of the Manitoba Indian Education Centre and a Winnipeg School Division employee. Activists describe the Urban Aboriginal Advisory Committee as an important avenue for Thunder Eagle Society as it worked within the system to support its aims. The group reported to the superintendent, and although it did not have any real authority, it did have some influence.

Following a long, sustained campaign led by Indigenous activists, in February 1990, the school division agreed in principle that it would assess the feasibility of an Aboriginal school. At this point there were several efforts to begin exploring different models. A "study tour group" that included Winnipeg School Division No.1 trustees, administrators, and others went to Calgary to visit the Plains Indian Cultural Survival School.

In a parallel effort, Larry Morrissette, David Blacksmith, and volunteer Thomas Saunders drove to Minneapolis-St. Paul, Minnesota with Community Education Development Association (CEDA) community worker Blair Hamilton. They wanted to learn about the Aboriginal Survival Schools established in that American state. There they visited several initiatives established by the American Indian Movement (AIM), including the Heart of the Earth and Red School House Aboriginal Survival Schools, a community training centre, as well as the AIM Patrol, which was the model for the first incarnation of the Bear Clan Patrol in Winnipeg.

Their host and guide was Mark Aquash, who has been described as a key figure in articulating how Indigenous education could be different.

Aquash was a PhD student and a member of AIM. The Survival schools were established by AIM to provide informal, supportive, culturally relevant learning environments for students who had struggled in the public schools. Survival school classes, for example, were often conducted with students and instructors seated together in a circle, which signified the concept of mutual human respect.[6] The curriculum integrated Indigenous cultural practices. Indigenous languages were also taught in the school. Others visited similar schools established in Vancouver, British Columbia, and Calgary, Alberta. Howard Green from the Native Education College in Vancouver was another respected advisor to the Aboriginal school activists.

Following this research, the activists formed a working group and drafted a proposal to establish an Aboriginal school in Winnipeg. It had become apparent from the dialogue with the Winnipeg School Division, and by looking at both the Minneapolis and Calgary models, that the school division would need a legal entity to negotiate with. A decision was taken to incorporate the Thunder Eagle Society as a democratic and accountable voice for the community. First incorporators were Larry Morrissette, Vern Morrissette, Wilfrid Buck, David Blacksmith, Bill Sanderson, and Eric Robinson.

In developing the proposal, the group was adamant that the school would be culturally rooted and that students would receive an education at the highest standards. They made clear that the school would not be a remedial school. They also agreed that they did not want the school to be a private, charter school but rather a school embedded in the public system through the Winnipeg School Division No.1. They believed strongly that education was a public responsibility. They also felt strongly in getting the best teachers possible, and to do so, they needed to ensure that they would be adequately paid and protected through the unionized environment of the public system.

6 Julie L. Davis, *Survival Schools: The American Indian Movement and Community Education in the Twin Cities* (Minneapolis: University of Minnesota Press, 2013).

In 1990, the Winnipeg School Division was still resistant to recognizing the Thunder Eagle Society as a legitimate community voice. As a strategic choice, the Thunder Eagle Society would eventually submit its proposal for an Aboriginal school to the Urban Aboriginal Advisory Committee so that the proposal could be submitted to the school division in the committee's name. The committee submitted the plan to the Winnipeg School Division Board of Trustees in January 1991. The Executive Summary of the proposal describes the need for an Aboriginal school as "substantiated by the long-term failure of the education system to meet the needs of Aboriginal children and youth."

The proposal describes "a first phase of a three-stage concept." It calls for a program for grades 9–12 involving 200 students. Future stages would see the development of Aboriginal schools for children in nursery school to grade 8.

The Executive Summary goes on to describe a school that would:

> Provide both general high school and university entrance courses. Aboriginal values will be integrated into every aspect of the school's teaching and operation. As well, there will be instruction in cultural practices, aboriginal languages, and activities of particular interest to Aboriginal students.
>
> The school will have 80% Aboriginal staff and the capacity to involve community people in the instruction related to cultural practices and activities. The school will be managed by a joint management committee with representatives from the student body, parents, Division administration, and a community society [Thunder Eagle Society]. The community society will serve as a democratic vehicle for all community people to be involved in setting a direction for the school. This society will legally contract with the Division to define roles and responsibilities.

The proposal also stipulates that:

> The budget for the school is at a comparable level to other high school programs of a similar size. The staffing configuration will also be comparable. Initially, the program will be located in an existing facility for the Division chosen by mutual arrangement.[7]

The proposal notes a process for curriculum development and states that "this school is a priority for the Urban Aboriginal Advisory Committee and should be considered a priority for the Board of Trustees."

The proposal was submitted in January 1991 and a few months later the division agreed to establish an Aboriginal school. In May 1991, the Thunder Eagle Society held a community meeting to elect its first board of directors. Bill Sanderson was elected as president. Sanderson brought a wealth of experience in the field of education and was the education director for Mathias Colomb Cree Nation at that time. In addition to the original incorporators, Virginia Maracle, Malvin St. Goddard, Jules Lavallee, Lawrence Guiboche, Charlotte Daniels, and Thomas Saunders were elected as directors. The Thunder Eagle Society Board established a staffing/hiring committee, curriculum committee, bylaws, and governance committee, and it moved quickly to develop a model of governance for the proposed Aboriginal High School.

After agreeing to establish an Aboriginal school in principle, the school division proposed three locations for the Aboriginal school. One location was the newly constructed Argyle Alternative School on Salter Street at Stella Avenue. Jerry Moore was the principal at Argyle School and a strong advocate for an Aboriginal school. He suggested that the Salter location was suitable and recommended that the school division relocate Argyle School to make room for the new Aboriginal school. Thunder Eagle Society and the Winnipeg School Division

7 Thunder Eagle Society, *A Proposal for an Aboriginal School*, submitted to the Winnipeg School Division Board of Trustees by the Urban Aboriginal Advisory Committee, January 18, 1991.

accepted this proposal. Jerry Moore and Argyle Alternative school relocated to Argyle Street.

The time leading up to and following the September 3 opening of Children of the Earth School was not easy for Thunder Eagle Society. Indigenous activists had long ago learned that nothing happened without a fight. As Vern Morrissette describes, "as always, we had to resort to something loud to get people to listen." The first battle was ensuring that the name of the school was changed on the building before its opening: "The Division was dragging its heels on that, so we did it ourselves." Activists took ladders to the school before its opening and physically changed the name themselves, removing Argyle from the sign and leaving "School" temporarily. When the school was officially named Children of the Earth School, the school division permanently changed the signage.

From the outset, there were struggles with the division over control, management, staffing and supports. For example, in June 1991, the president of Thunder Eagle Society sent a letter to the inner-city superintendent of Winnipeg School Division No.1, formally requesting a community school coordinator to engage community involvement. The letter noted the Thunder Eagle Society's interest in Susie Martin, a community school coordinator employed by CEDA placed in another inner-city school. A month later the superintendent declined the request in writing, noting that "within the existing contract with CEDA there is no additional time available to be assigned to the Aboriginal High School."[8] It isn't clear from records and interviews what discussions took place after the letter was received, but CEDA eventually placed Susie Martin at the school.

On June 28, 1991, the Thunder Eagle board unanimously approved a Model of Governance developed by the Governance Committee. It was agreed that the model would be presented to the Urban Aboriginal

8 Letter from Pauline Clarke, Superintendent of Schools Inner City to Bill Sanderson, President, Thunder Eagle Society. July 4, 1991. available at the the University of Manitoba Archives and Special Collections. Winnipeg, MB.

Advisory Committee with the intent to table it before the Program Policy Committee of the school board. In a letter dated September 23, 1991, the school division's chief superintendent, J. C. Smyth, wrote that although the school division agreed with much of the content of the proposal,

> the format and certain provisions are of some difficulty to us. We feel that there has been good cooperation in the establishment and operation of the school to this point in time and we have every intention of ensuring that this cooperation continues. We do, however, feel that this school year will result in a review of many areas of operation of the school and a more formal document, if required, would be more appropriately considered after the completion of the 1991–92 school year.[9]

Attached to the letter was a revised set of guidelines for the operation of the school. The document narrowed the role of the "joint management committee" proposed by Thunder Eagle Society. Thunder Eagle wanted the joint management committee to "be involved in all staffing decisions." They made clear that they wanted "decision making powers."

Nonetheless, the Division would maintain power as laid out in the revised guidelines. The new model included two members of the Thunder Eagle Society on a School Management Committee of ten members. The role of the committee was to "consult with and provide advice to the principal." Although they could provide "advice" about the hiring of teachers, course offerings, spending priorities, and other policies, they did not have any real power in the decision-making process.

The two entities later came to an agreement, and on January 16, 1992, the Thunder Eagle Society and the Winnipeg School Division No.1 signed a Joint Statement and Declaration of Intent and Objectives Agreement. While the Winnipeg School Division held ultimate power,

9 J. C. Smyth letter to Larry Morrissette September 23, 1991, available at the the University of Manitoba Archives and Special Collections. Winnipeg, Mb.

the role of the community in this school, through Thunder Eagle Society, far exceeded what was the norm in other Winnipeg School Division schools. The joint agreement acknowledged the society's mission "to promote the integration of Aboriginal culture and values into all aspects of the school program." The Thunder Eagle Society had achieved a significant and historical milestone. Despite the resistance of the school division, the community succeeded in doing what it set out to do. Establish *"a school of our own...a place where we can go to be with our own people and learn in our own way."*

In October 1991, three members resigned from the board (Maracle, Lavallee, and Daniels) and were replaced by Gwen Merrick, Helen Thundercloud, and Agnes Brass. In 1992 the Thunder Eagle Society held its second elections. Having come under criticism for the lack of women representation, the new board included five men (Brad Beach, Ron Castel, Michael Hart, Morris Hart, Larry Morrissette) and eight women (Agnes Brass, Donna Everette, Susie Martin, Catherine Richard, Marguerita Roberts, Eleanor Robertson, Priscilla Settee, Helen Thundercloud and Children of the Earth principal, Mary Courchene.)

Mary Courchene was the first principal of Children of the Earth School. As principal of the school, she worked closely with Thunder Eagle Society and sat on the Joint Management Committee. She had previously been a teacher at R.B. Russell School on Dufferin Avenue. In an interview with Larry Morrissette in 2013, Courchene recalled that as a teacher in the system, she could not actively engage with activists. She saw her role as being supportive behind the scenes. She said she believed strongly in the need for an Aboriginal school steeped in cultural traditions. She also said that she encouraged her students to participate in the youth/elder workshops at the Freight House led by Larry Morrissette and Wilfred Buck.

When Children of the Earth School was established, Courchene applied to be a teacher. She was accepted but was soon appointed as principal. Courchene had gained experience as a school administrator in Sagkeeng First Nation, so she seemed a logical choice and was offered the position. Her appointment as principal was also somewhat serendipitous; the person who initially received the—and who had accepted the position—withdrew their application in July 1991, just two months before the school was to open. Courchene recalled having been given "one night to think about it." After consulting with an elder and her family, she accepted the position. She describes being "not too sure what was expected of me" as the first Aboriginal principal of the new Aboriginal school, but she knew that it was the right thing to do.

Mary Courchene describes her first-day meeting at Children of the Earth School with the Division Superintendent:

> ...so I go into this school, brand new school...brand new building, there was not a thing inside that building, not one desk, nothing... and this was in the middle of July. So we only had from that time to the end of August to get ready for this, this grand opening. And he said, well, you'll have your community to help you.[10]

At a meeting of the Thunder Eagle Society in 1992, Courchene, now the principal of Children of the Earth School, described to the group several ongoing conflicts between the school division and the Thunder Eagle Society. Principal Courchene emphasized to the group that she identified first and foremost as an Aboriginal person and had mostly been able to resolve conflicts with the school division.[11] But she made clear that the active support from Thunder Eagle Society was greatly needed in the following areas:

1. Thunder Eagle Society to provide overall direction of the school.
2. Thunder Eagle Society to provide direction regarding the overall cultural program.

10 Mary Courchene, interview by Larry Morrissette, 7 March, 2013. Recording at the the University of Manitoba Archives and Special Collections. Winnipeg, MB.

11 Thunder Eagle Society Workshop, "Toward a Common Vision," February 8–9, 1992, unpublished notes available at the University of Manitoba Archives.

3. The Joint Management Committee to report to the Thunder Eagle Society and receive direction from the Society.
4. Thunder Eagle Society to act as a political lobby group to ensure the needs of Children of the Earth School.
5. Thunder Eagle Society to lobby for more autonomy in the school including greater power and input from the community versus the school division.
6. Greater presence of Thunder Eagle Society in day-to-day operations.[12]

Thunder Eagle Society continued to fight for resources for the school. They felt that the administration was intentionally making it difficult. But they also had many teachers on their side. Former president of the board at Thunder Eagle Society Bill Sanderson recalls that teachers like Donna Delaronde and Debbie Beach were very vocal in their demand for resources, including furniture, Indigenous books for the library, and basic supplies. But they also needed allies in the school division.

Strategies and Allies: School Trustees and the Urban and Aboriginal Advisory Committee

The early decision to shepherd the proposal for an Aboriginal school through the Urban and Aboriginal Advisory Committee proved to be a strategic move for the Thunder Eagle Society. Although the Aboriginal Advisory Committee did not have power itself, it was able to work within the system to help move the community vision forward. The advisory committee was established following a recommendation by the Task Force on Race Relations in a 1989 report to the school division. The task force was established in 1988 by the trustees of the Winnipeg School Division No.1. The purpose of the task force, made up of trustees, administrators, educators, and community members, was to "develop policies and recommendations in the matters of race and

12 Ibid.

ethnicity as they relate to the student programs, curriculum, the assessment and placement of students in classes for exceptional children, staff professional development, community relations, recreational programs, equal opportunity and the handling of racial incidents."[13]

Thunder Eagle Society realized that they could get further traction if they had political support and allies within the school division. The Urban and Aboriginal Advisory Committee was critical to the society's early success. This success motivated the community to organize and elect Indigenous community members as school trustees. In 1992, they were successful in their efforts to elect Bill Sanderson (former chair of the Thunder Eagle Society) and Kathy Mallett (long-time community activist) as school trustees. Sanderson and Mallett describe their time as school trustees as challenging, frustrating, and time-consuming. Although the community rallied to get them elected, they remember feeling a "bit on our own" once elected. While they developed some allies during their three years as trustees, racism at the school board was prevalent, albeit subtle. Despite being university educated, Sanderson and Mallett said they were often treated as "dummies," and other trustees were very much resistant to the Aboriginal schools.

Vern Morrissette also remembers facing resistance, but he and others also acknowledge that support for the Aboriginal schools grew. They note support from, in particular, non-Indigenous trustees Lionel Orlikow, Irene Haigh, and Anita Neville. Non-Indigenous trustees Roman Yereniuk and MaryAnn Mihychuk slowly came on board, while Ed Kowalchuk, Mario Santos, and Betty Granger remained resistant. Indigenous trustees Mallett and Sanderson worked with the Urban Aboriginal Advisory Committee and non-Indigenous ally trustees to build support for the Aboriginal schools. They also worked to ensure that Indigenous teachers were promoted into leadership roles. Thirteen teachers were promoted during their time as trustees. They also note

13 Winnipeg School Division, *The Report of The Task Force on Race Relations to the Board of Trustees of The Winnipeg School Division No.1*, 1989.

the support of Jerry Moore, the principal of Argyle School that would become the location of Children of the Earth School.

Soon after Children of the Earth School was established, Thunder Eagle Society began to pursue the next stage of its vision—an elementary school. They set their sights on Aberdeen School, adjacent to Children of the Earth School on Flora Avenue. With the precedent of Children of the Earth High School, convincing the school division to establish an Aboriginal elementary school was less of a challenge. But they still had to convince the school division and trustees, and they still faced some resistance. Some trustees and division bureaucrats thought that an Aboriginal program could be included in the existing school and program. The community won that fight, adamant that the school itself needed to be transformed into an Aboriginal school in the same way that Children of the Earth School had been. Some trustees and school division bureaucrats were resistant to a name change. Thunder Eagle Society, with the support of the community, was adamant that the name also needed to change. At a community event organized by Thunder Eagle Society to discuss the school's future, only one individual spoke to his concerns about renaming the school. He had no support. Approximately 300 people in attendance took a vote and all but one person voted to establish the school as an Aboriginal school and rename it Niji Mahkwa (my friend the bear).

Soon after Niji Mahkwa school opened, the Thunder Eagle Society slowly dissolved. Those we spoke with do not recall a definitive moment or event that precipitated its demise. Like many activist organizations, Thunder Eagle Society was born of a sense of urgency to advocate for a particular issue. Despite the best of intentions, it was a volunteer organization with little capacity to fully engage in the day-to-day operations of the school. When Thunder Eagle Society achieved its goals and Children of the Earth and Niji Mahkwa schools were established, the sense of urgency dissipated, and the community moved on to organize around other urgent issues. Community members have continued to engage with the school, but the need for the legal structure that became the Thunder Eagle Society was no longer necessary. It had essentially been created as a means to an end. Activists responded to the school division's inability or unwillingness to see the activists as a legitimate representation of the community.

Children of the Earth and Niji Mahkwa schools have been part of the North End community for more than thirty years. They are important symbols of Winnipeg's history of Indigenous resistance and development, yet few people know how they came to be. Reflecting on that time, Vern Morrissette tells his brother Larry,

> I'm humbled to have been part of that history. It was an amazing time for Aboriginal activism...based in an Aboriginal understanding of what we had to do.
>
> We learned early on how to be activists even before Children of the Earth and Niiji Makwa. We didn't know we were activists.
>
> When I was fourteen years old, we learned to fight. We wanted a place to call our own and to hang out, and we established the Community Action Centre, which eventually was taken out of our hands and gentrified. The activism was in our community. It came from a good place and it came from a bad place—we wanted to be ourselves—it came from the anger and the oppression that we felt. We all carried the scars of residential schools.
>
> The most important thing...maintain our identity. Remember the qualities of our ancestors. [Otherwise] we will lose our way...
>
> People don't know the full story...We got it, we got a school—Children of the Earth High School—and we were so proud and we were so happy. Unless you [tell the] history, it gets lost.
>
> Children of the Earth and Niji Mahkwa schools are now well-established "places of our own," spaces of hope for Indigenous children to be themselves and maintain their identities as proud Indigenous people. Some of those children have become and will become the next generation of activists, continuing the fight for justice for those to follow.

Bibliography

Courchene, Mary. Interview by Larry Morrissette, 2013.

Davis, Julie L. *Survival Schools: The American Indian Movement and Community Education in the Twin Cities.* Minneapolis: University of Minnesota Press, 2013.

Morrissette, Vern. Interview by Larry Morrissette, 2013.

Niji Mahkwa School. https://www.winnipegsd.ca/nijimahkwa/page/6570/our-visionWinnipeg School Division. Accessed January 28, 2023.

Smyth, J. C. letter to Larry Morrissette September 23, 1991, available at the the University of Manitoba Archives and Special Collections. Winnipeg, MB.

Thunder Eagle Society. *A Proposal for an Aboriginal School. Submitted to the Winnipeg School Division Board of Trustees by the Urban Aboriginal Advisory Committee.* January 18, 1991.

Thunder Eagle Society Workshop. "Toward a Common Vision." February 8–9, 1992. Unpublished notes available at the University of Manitoba Archives.

Winnipeg School Division. *The Report of The Task Force on Race Relations to the Board of Trustees of The Winnipeg School Division No.1.* 1989.

Chapter 6

The Indigenous Women's Collective of Manitoba:

DIBENIMISOWIN (We Own Ourselves)

Doris Young

BACKGROUND DESCRIPTION

This chapter provides a brief history of the Indigenous Women's Collective of Manitoba (IWC), including its development and formation. It is also a memoir of one of the women who participated in the creation and leadership of the organization for many years. The IWC was composed of Indigenous women, including Status, Non-Status, and Métis women. Its main objective was to be the political voice for Aboriginal women in Manitoba on issues affecting their political, economic, social, language, and legal rights. There were many concerns confronting Aboriginal women in the early 1980s, and community groups were formed to find solutions. These community groups had strong female leadership but concluded that working in isolation from each other was not effective. In 1984, representatives of the community groups attended a Manitoba Aboriginal women's conference where they voted to form a political organization that would unite their efforts under one umbrella organization. The IWC developed bylaws and became incorporated in 1985. Although the IWC was a provincial organization, its formation took place in Winnipeg. Its regional office was Winnipeg based for accessibility.

An Idea from an Old Tradition

The year was 1984. I found myself standing in a conference room at the Marlborough Hotel in Winnipeg, Manitoba. I had been invited to the Aboriginal Women's Annual Conference as a delegate. Standing by the doorway, I stopped for a few minutes to look in awe at all the beautiful Aboriginal women who had come together at this conference. There was one woman I particularly remember. She wore a bright red dress and a beaded jacket. She spoke with confidence and power. I will never forget what a dynamic woman she was and how the group gathered around her listening to her words. I thought perhaps one day, I could be that confident. But first…

I am an Ininiw iskeiwrom the Opaskwayak Cree Nation (OCN), the Treaty 5 area in northern Manitoba where we have lived as Cree people for as long as memory serves us. Our territory is dotted with many lakes and rivers, the woods, the swamps which form part of the Boreal Forest. Our medicines came from this land, as did our economy, our livelihood, as well as our language, our laws, and our governing systems. This amazing area provided everything we needed to live a good life. We practiced Midewewin (a medicine society) before contact; we did ceremonies like the goose dance which no one hardly remembers now. It is a ceremony to welcome the geese back each spring and fall. Everyone loved spring and fall when the geese returned to our land. Other ceremonies healed the sick and blessed the new babies that arrived. This land is special. This land gives us life.

As a very young child, I remember my earlier, happy days at Opaskwayak. We were loved and well taken care of. I especially cherish the memories of my grandmother and her kindness. She was blind and I never knew her to be able to see us, but she knew if we were too thin and made sure we ate more. This safety and comfort all changed for me by being forcibly sent to two residential schools. After residential school, I was never again able to fully capture the safety I knew as a child. Being removed from my home and my community left a deep scar in my heart, and the trauma has never really gone away. I have learned to live with this consequence, and I drew upon my community's gentleness to help stabilize me, and I turned to advocacy work. We formed a community women's group to talk about OCN issues and to focus on solutions. The Opaskwayak Women's Group had long been concerned about two main issues: our membership issues where our sisters were losing their treaty status upon marriage to Non-Treaty men,[1] and our residential school experiences. Both of these issues adversely affected our community. Our sisters who married Non-Treaty men were not living with us anymore. We missed them and we worried about them and their children's health and safety. Many of us had been forced as children to go to residential schools approximately 800 kilometers and more away from OCN. We were badly mistreated at these schools, plus the loss of children growing up in our community severely affected all families. We acknowledged the injustice of these coercive laws and policies and joined our sisters nationally in addressing the membership issue. Residential Schools would later become a major national issue.

Back to the Winnipeg conference. Here was a roomful of women who came to share their experiences and to make changes in our lives. There were First Nations, Non-Status, Métis and Inuit women who came from communities throughout Manitoba, including Winnipeg. We came from wide geographical areas throughout Manitoba, which included many remote northern communities. I, along with many of the delegates, lived in northern Manitoba's First Nations and Métis

1 The Numbered Treaties are international diplomatic agreements with the Crown to protect the land and ensure First Nation sovereignty, nationhood, and way of life. Rights from the Treaties include education, economic development, and health services. Treaty people are members of a First Nation whose descendants signed Treaties.

communities (Appendix 1). The only way of getting in and out of some communities was by airplane. Other delegates lived in rural and urban settings, including Winnipeg. Many were single parents (including myself) struggling to make daily ends meet. We were mothers, grandmothers, midwives, professors, teachers, nurses, doctors, traditional medicine women, elders, community workers. These women were also my friends, my family members, my mentors, and my elders. We greeted each other in friendship and love. In our greetings, we shared our yearly news with one another. Some stories were sad and disturbing. We hugged those women who had sad stories. Some stories were funny, and we laughed with those women and hugged again. I felt like I belonged. I was honoured and excited to be there.

As mentioned earlier, many of us had lived through residential school abuses, most of the women had felt the ugly sting of racism, and many had lost their First Nations status because they married non–First Nations men. Some had experienced the Sixties Scoop era. The Sixties Scoop was so named for that period of the 1960s when provincial child welfare agencies indiscriminately picked up (scooped up) Aboriginal children they considered neglected. Most were not neglected but were economically poor and society considered this unacceptable. Other issues Aboriginal women faced were inadequate health services, and lack of employment and decent housing. All these conditions caused us pain as they were unjust and demeaning.

This was not the first time that any of us had participated in Aboriginal women's conferences, but this was an "ah ha" moment. This was a historic conference. There was something important in the air at that conference, something that would move us into united action and unity. Our discussions took us to the essential need to form a Manitoba Aboriginal women's organization.

Organizing to Become a Political Organization

That year we had come together as we did each year to talk about our communities, our future as women, and the future of our children.

It was special. We realized that these same issues were discussed every year with hardly any resolution. Yearly conferences were nice, but they were not getting our problems resolved. Small individual community groups by themselves were not strong enough to make changes.

The conference discussions led us to conclude that if we united under one umbrella, we could achieve results. We recognized that a large, strong body—a political body—would make a difference. We talked about an organization that could stand firm together, one that would work toward making the social, political, and legal changes we needed. This was the historical moment for Manitoba Aboriginal women to unite and work together in partnership and in solidarity. Our common issues unified us. I cannot remember which group made the recommendation to form an organization composed of all the women's groups at that conference; however, the idea caught on fire. We believed that if our joint cluster organizations united as a group, they would be able to make that difference. With that said, the next day, a decision was made to elect a leader to help lead us to fulfill our purposes.

The Leadership Selection Process

It didn't take long to organize the process for electing a leadership—women are great strategists and organizers. We were Aboriginal women who had just decided to form our own women's organization. It was exciting. The air was filled with hope and a promise as fresh as a spring day. We decided we would not vote along community or political lines. The unique point of the process was that we were not voting for our particular organization's candidate. There was no talk about our affiliate organization as being the best choice. We were voting to pick the best candidate for a leader. The process would be one vote for each woman. The election would take place the next day. If there was lobbying that evening, it was done with kindness and respect for one another. Our group—the Opaskwayak Women's Group—didn't discuss the election. We went for supper and talked about our communities, our grandmothers, and our children. As usual, there was a lot of laughter and good visiting.

On Election Day, there was excitement in the air. I recall the lineup at the polling booths. There had been no speech made; there had only been names presented for a candidate and a time for the process the next day. I think there were three candidates. We were all enthusiastic, but I was also apprehensive; my name was on the ballot as a presidential candidate. The line moved quickly. I believe there were two rounds. I thought that one of the other two candidates would be our best choice. I was nervous and overwhelmed when I became the first elected president of the IWC. I remember clearly that I was so scared of the responsibility that I wanted to refuse this elected status. I went to a quiet spot and wondered about this leadership position. *Could I do it? Should I take on this task? Did I want to?* I now was not the woman who a few days ago stood in the doorway peering in; I was asked to come in and lead these women on a journey that was not only exciting but also full of potholes and obstacles. I knew our issues were important, our children's futures were important, *we* were important. Their trust in me was daunting.

I remembered all the women who helped make changes. To name a few: Dr. Verna Kirkness, who contributed to the policy paper *Indian Control of Indian Education* that started us on a road of demanding Aboriginal educational changes across the country.[2] Dorothy McKay, who was the first Winnipeg executive director of the Indian and Métis Friendship Centre; Dorothy Settee, who worked tirelessly keeping Cree alive at schools, interpreting at hospitals, and going wherever she was needed; Flora Zaharia, the Aboriginal education giant in

2 National Indian Brotherhood/Assembly of First Nations, *Indian Control of Indian Education*, policy paper presented to the Minister of Indian Affairs and Northern Development (Ottawa: National Indian Brotherhood/Assembly of First Nations, 1972), https://oneca.com/IndianControlofIndianEducation.pdf.

the province's education system; and Elder Eva McKay, a strong and thoughtful leader at the Sioux Valley First Nation. These were some of our exceptional and brilliant leaders. They were trailblazers and my mentors. I was not alone, but I had big shoes to fill. After deep contemplation and "looking back and looking forward" at our issues and the reasons for our new organization, the answer came back "yes" to all three questions. *Yes, I would do it, yes, I would take on this task, and yes, I wanted to.* My doubts vanished and I felt confident that we would become a dynamic group. I trusted that the women would come through on their obligations to our organization too. Leadership was, after all, in the hands of all of us—not just one woman. Also after all, the essence of our new organization was our determination to work together with the values of caring, respect, sharing, love, being brave, truth-telling. These long-held values would help us accomplish the work of advocating for justice and equality. We did not yet have an organizational name; that would come later.

Naming the Organization

Manitoba's First Nations, Métis, Inuit, Non-Status and Status women voted to unite under an umbrella organization and for a new leader. A committee was tasked with providing suggestions to name our organization. They were given a year to fulfill this responsibility. At the next conference, various names and the reason for their suitability were presented. There was debate and thoughtful contemplation regarding these suggestions. Based on the committee's excellent recommendations, we unanimously decided that our newly minted organization would be called the Manitoba Indigenous Women's Collective (IWC). The name was appropriate for our organization. We were, after all, a collective of Manitoba Aboriginal women's groups united in work for the children of tomorrow. The IWC was later incorporated as a political organization and became the Indigenous Women's Collective Inc. with bylaws. Our collective included the family and the community claiming respect and a dignified life for all, because we understood that dignifying ourselves and our people is a significant mission. Mere survival was not a solution; cultural, social, economic, and political diversity for ourselves with justice as a cornerstone were important principles.

Defining Strategies

Forming a Manitoba Aboriginal women's organization was our first item—our first accomplishment. Our organizational goals were about equity and social justice, and to the membership, our goals were accountability, accessibility, and transparency. We pondered our other strategies and reflected on the colonial interruption of our original roles.

We chose to work with grassroots agendas and communicate these issues to provincial and federal governments through meetings, correspondence, and demonstrations if need be. We chose to create partnerships with allies such as other Aboriginal organizations and non-Aboriginal groups for support; to create partnerships and collaborate on issues when necessary; and to present briefs to the Senate, the provincial and federal parliament as applicable. Mentorship and funding were priorities for the organization. The IWC operated without funding for the first four years. We were all unpaid workers; most of us held down two jobs—one paid and one unpaid. We had small children to consider while still maintaining the organization. Our support of one another was our pillar. Even without finances, Aboriginal women were determined to break the silence of our situations and move forward for improvement in our lives. The women were strong. The women were committed, and we were unwavering in purpose.

During those earlier IWC days, Manitoba Aboriginal women began to reawaken to the sound of our drums, to stand tall while listening to and responding to our own voices. We were determined to succeed. We realized that all decisions made by governments affect society in some way or another, and the effects of these decisions on Aboriginal women were glaring. We worked on defining our issues to make them political. Women worked in their communities during the year and attended the yearly IWC Annual General Assemblies (AGA), and each community sent delegates to represent their area. The AGA was a time for reunion and a place for making "to do" lists for the following year through resolutions. Each community group sat together to discuss their issues and present them in either a resolution for action or information only. As usual, each woman had a vote on the issues of next year's "to do" list. One of our funding proposals was approved, and we were able to hire an executive director in year two. Our first executive director was a dynamic woman, Joan Alex from Berens River, Manitoba. Alex later became a lawyer and is still an active advocate. She kept us busy, and we were all grateful for her good, strong energy in keeping us on track with our work.

Mamawi and Whakotowin

(Cree words for working together through positive respectful relationships, strength, support, and partnership)

> *"Leadership is about service, giving voice to every woman; participation and contribution is absolutely necessary to be whole, it's not about counting the cost before being involved; sacrifices are made to move the issues forward."*—Maureen Brown, OCN Onuschekew (council member).

During the year, we stayed in touch through respectful relationships. Whakotowin was maintained by telephone conversations, meetings when finances allowed, and by correspondence. We kept our relationships alive through any means that were available to us. There was a feeling of togetherness that made the organization work in a unified and caring way.

The IWC often helped with writing proposals to fund community projects and with fundraising community activities. Each community knew they would be supported when required. One of our more exciting fundraising projects was to raise finances to attend the World Conference of Women in Moscow in 1987, and ten excited women were able to attend—me being one of them.

Mentorship was provided to young people to help them prepare research applications and investigate issues. They also received mentorship to help them develop skills in proposal writing and in preparing briefs for Senate and other political presentations. We encouraged the young researchers to make presentations to voice their concerns at the provincial and federal levels. Part of the mentorship platform was to mentor young women to take on leadership roles, so it was decided that each president would only serve four years, and that each outgoing president would provide support to the new president as needed.

The Indigenous Women's Collective of Manitoba Inc. (IWC) was a daunting development considering that powerful male Aboriginal political organizations were already in place: that is, the First Nations organizations the Assembly of Manitoba Chiefs Manitoba (AMC), Manitoba Keewatinook Okimakanak (MKO), Manitoba Tribal Councils, as well as the Manitoba Métis Federation (MMF) and its various locals. The IWC worked to become allies with these organizations. We supported their efforts and still moved forward with ours. We were politically united.

Atoskewin—Learning and Leading

(Cree word for working)

> *"In our Aboriginal way, we learn to listen from our earliest days. We could not live good and useful lives unless we listened. It was the normal way for us to learn—not by asking questions. We learned by watching and listening, waiting and then acting. Our people have passed on this way of listening for over 40,000 years... "*[3]—Miriam Rose Ungunmerr-Baumann

I learned leadership from my mother and father. My mother raised fifteen children and had to know how to organize, plan, and lead. She

3 Frank Brennan and Miriam Rose Ungunmerr-Bauman, "Reverencing the Earth in the Australian Dreaming," *The Way* 29, 1 (1997): 38–45.

organized our work schedules when we were home. She organized our winter's trapping food supplies, our clothing needs, her medicines that we would need during the long winter months when we were in a very isolated area. None of these were easy chores. She had to devise a system so that nothing was forgotten. She started organizing mid-summer. Winters were harsh, and trapping areas were far from towns. Our lives depended on her organizational skills. She taught us our culture, our language, her plant knowledge.

My mother also often had tea and bannock and an afternoon of talk with the women about the community and what was happening and what required attention. The women would talk about the needs of the elders and the children. Who needs food? Who needs water? (Most of our northern communities did not have potable drinking water.) Who needs wood? Who needs medical attention? As for the children, there was talk of who was out too late and who was being rude and what could be done about these situations. She worked with mothers and grandmothers to make the "to do" list. In the end, my mother would relay this list as action items to my father for OCN Council work. Of course, we know that unless issues are brought to the table, nothing gets done. Women played those crucial roles of ensuring action and accountability. Aboriginal women were the force behind the men who were our elected leaders.

My father was Onekanew (leader) in my community, and as a young person, I listened and watched his style of leadership too. Community needs were met through the following process: the heart feels the issues, the head processes with thoughts of how to execute, the hands were where action happened.This was his leadership process. As Onekanew, his job was to present the issues, and together the Council would find solutions. Decisions were always about meeting community needs. My dad always worked with Council and together they found solutions.

And I also learned that leadership decisions and actions are based on community—the people's needs. It seemed to me that the process of *heart* > *head* > *hand* > was where *action* was achieved. The action started from the heart (an issue that needed attention was felt by the heart—for example, an elder couple needs wood); heart feels this circumstance from the talk at the meeting; head listens, and a procedure is designed of what to do (find someone to get wood to the elders); and the hand—action follows. The wood is delivered by the person who has been delegated to do the work. A community need is met. The Council has fulfilled a need; the elders are happy and will be warm. All is ok.

There is also another process that I observed that involved *follow > lead*; *lead > follow*. The leader (Onekanew) followed community direction and sometimes led the way (for example, negotiating with the Indian Agent in our communities as most issues had to be approved by that "watch dog"). My father would be the negotiator, depending on the issue. Sometimes he was not familiar with an issue so another Council member who had the expertise of that topic would be the leader at the negotiation meeting. No one made a fuss about a person leading an issue. Permission was given to the one who had the knowledge and the ability to lead in a particular circumstance. This was true leadership as I saw it, and together—always together regardless of who was leading—a situation was fixed. The way things got done seemed simple enough. The process was passed down through generations, honouring and delivering. It served every leader very well throughout the generations. Aboriginal women know that process. I would carry out that practice within the IWC.

Governing—Dibenimisowin

> *"When you hear, you awaken. That is for your heart.*
> *When you feel, it becomes part of you. That is for your spirit.*
> *It is so you learn to listen with your whole being.*
> *That is how you learn."*[4]
> —Richard Wagamese

4 Richard Wagamese, *Embers: One Ojibway's Meditations* (Madeira Park, BC: Douglas and McIntyre, 2016), 113.

I also relied on other Cree principles of governing from my earliest days of going to Band Council meetings with my father. Principles that were based on culture, Traditional Knowledge, and historical connection. The principles placed within our central selves, a vision and purpose of what it means to "own ourselves." Dibenimisowin means "owning ourselves" in Cree and doing it "our way" because it is the right way for us. We worked to transform this vision into action-for-us at that time. "Dibenimisowin—that's who and what we are," an elder at a Council meeting said as she talked about an important Cree law on governing. She also said, "Creator put us on this earth with everything that we need to be able to care for ourselves: intelligence, land, language, laws, governments, institutions, families, children. We lead ourselves because we have the authority to do that." We look forward and think about our actions on Seven Generations and beyond. Looking Seven Generations and beyond is important because the children of tomorrow will benefit (or suffer) from our actions of today. From Dibenimisowin comes Mino Bimatisiwin. Mino Bimatisiwn in Cree means "to have a good life," and when we own ourselves, we do what we need to do to be healthy and safe, in all matters related to the nation. The IWC worked for healthy communities and healthy people.

Issues: IWC Membership

IWC strengthened membership by enrolling women who came to the meetings each year as delegates from their various communities. All delegates were willing to support the IWC by becoming members, and the process ensured that our membership was province-wide and expanded each year. I do not have a membership record, but we enrolled women every year from the various members who came to the conferences, and we could prove that our membership and our work were solely based in Winnipeg. I believe that IWC was eventually granted core funding from the provincial government because it had established a strong healthy working relationship with affiliated community groups. In the process, our members defined our province-wide agenda. Although core funding greatly enhanced the organization's urban-based political ability, it came at a price for northern and rural communities to effectively participate.

Inadequate funding made northern and rural concerns problematic. The province-wide agenda became urban based, and eventually issues could not be reconciled. Membership dropped off, financial issues were probed, and eventually funding for IWC was terminated.

Colonization: The Residential School System and the Sixties Scoop and Child Welfare

IWC membership came from historic lines whose beautiful, strong, and functional cultures stem from generations back. In pre-colonial times, women directed the leadership (as illustrated earlier). This governing practice was passed down from generation to generation, from grandmother to mother to daughter. Women's authority and support came from their sacred laws and traditional systems. The nation supported and respected Aboriginal women's authority. In their roles, women were devoted to their work and dedicated to their families and community. Western colonial laws and policies usurped and upset these traditional spiritual, political, and legal responsibilities. Aboriginal women were left without position or authority.

The federal government legislated Indian residential schools and authorized church and state to remove children from their homes to be educated by the churches. The Truth and Reconciliation Commission estimated that 150,000 children were removed from their homes over a 150-year period.[5] The Provincial Child Welfare law and policies sanctioned the infamous Sixties Scoop where child welfare workers illegally scooped up Métis children and placed them into the provincial child

5 From *Honouring the Truth, Reconciling for the Future.* Summary of the Final Report of the Truth and Reconciliation Commission of Canada. The Truth and Reconciliation Commission of Canada. https://nctr.ca/records/reports/#trc-reports.

welfare system. Children were placed into white foster homes and/or adopted nationally and internationally by white families. Many of these children never returned home. Some returned but never really fit, culturally; they were neither Métis nor white. In both the residential school and the child welfare systems, parents lost control of raising their children. Aboriginal women as the "carriers of the culture" had traditionally taught their children to be strong and proud Aboriginal women and men. Through a colonial process, Aboriginal education and the transmission of Aboriginal culture and language were no longer permitted.

But traditions are hard to break and eradicate entirely. In their homes, Aboriginal women carried out their duties. In their hearts, the flame smoldered as they went about their daily work, waiting for the right time to act. Hearts were relentless in their desire to restore their rights as mothers. The residential schools were closed by the end of the 1990s, but parenting skills were already severely fragmented, and many First Nations children were taken into the provincial child welfare system. The IWC wrote petitions, demonstrated, and marched on the provincial legislature, demanding the transfer of provincial control to Aboriginal control. Our brother organizations marched with us, and we all made demands to Manitoba to stop taking our children.

One Step Forward, Two Steps Back

Provincial child welfare laws were opened up to allow Aboriginal child care workers to administer provincial child welfare in Manitoba.[6] We were exceedingly joyful with this victory, but our joy soon turned into some very large disappointments. We could not foresee the problems that would arise from Aboriginal people taking over the administration of the child welfare system. We did not realize that Aboriginal

6 Judge E.C. Kimelman, *No Quiet Place: Review Committee on Indian and Métis Adoption and Placements* (Winnipeg: Manitoba Department of Community Service and Corrections, 1985).

agencies were not in a position to begin administering Aboriginal cultural child care. Adequate administrative funding and staff training in Aboriginal cultural practices were two important needs that were not met. Many of the child welfare workers were intergenerational residential school children. Aboriginal child-rearing practices that their mothers and grandmothers knew were not handed down to them because of residential schools and the Sixties Scoop era. We had expected that Aboriginal child care workers would be able to step into this administrative role with Aboriginal knowledge on Aboriginal child care practices.

Another issue: in order to practice and be employed as social workers, they had to upgrade their skills. They were required to attend education systems like the School of Social Work at the University of Manitoba or other social work programs in Canada. The university educators only taught white child-care cultural norms and provincial child welfare policies. Also, funding for these programs had to come from the Aboriginal child-caring agencies who were not funded for these education programs. As a result, colonial child welfare practices and policies became even more entrenched. But this time, Aboriginal people were enforcing and administering these laws. Freedom from the colonizers and our right to raise our children openly slipped out of our hands. Today in Manitoba, more Aboriginal children are in this child welfare system than in any other province. There is one tiny light at the end of this tunnel: today, the University of Manitoba in the Master of Social Work has an Indigenous Knowledge (IK) program. The MSW-IK program teaches Aboriginal child-caring practices, and Aboriginal students are given priority to enter the program. But this is a more recent curriculum, and in 1985 this was only a dream.

Discrimination

The Indian Act also took away the rights of First Nations women to retain First Nation status when marrying a non–First Nations man.

With the stroke of a pen, she also lost her treaty rights to education, to health services, and to live in her community. She also could not pass her rights down to her children. Men, on the other hand, who married non–First Nations women, gained all these rights, and the non–First Nations women were passing these rights down to their children. Jeanette Corbiere Lavalle went to court claiming discrimination. After losing her battle at the provincial level, in 1983, the highest Canadian court, the Supreme Court of Canada, ruled in her favour. The 1985 amendment to the Indian Act, which was generally referred to as Bill C-31, declared that First Nations women could no longer lose their treaty status upon marriage.

Education, Employment, and Training

Many Aboriginal people found it difficult to complete school due to an education system that refused to acknowledge Aboriginal knowledge, history, and experience. They lagged behind in education, and low education achievement was reflected in workforce statistics. In 1985, three quarters of the Aboriginal population in Winnipeg alone had less than Grade 11 education.[7] This statistic would probably present a much lower rate for Aboriginal women and for the rural and northern Aboriginal populations. Aboriginal people had fewer employment and training opportunities. Many Aboriginal people did not have work experience that could enhance their ability to find employment. Training programs were out of reach for many with lower academic credentials. Many employees were prejudiced against hiring Aboriginal people due to racist stereotyping. There was a high number of single mothers (including myself) who faced their own set of problems, as child care facilities were just not available. This was the situation for most Aboriginal women in the early 1980s.

The IWC did not solve most employment problems for Aboriginal women; however, overall employment strategies, resources for training

7 John Loxley, in 1996 report to the Royal Commission on Aboriginal People.

programs, and supports in skills development to further careers became available. This was partly as a result of Aboriginal political efforts, including those of the IWC. IWC contributed to empowering and strengthening Aboriginal women in the workforce. Its economic development ventures helped more Aboriginal women find jobs. The IWC moved into training programs and some women ventured into economic development, running their own businesses: Neechi Foods, a food store in Winnipeg's North End, and some arts and crafts businesses are examples. Comprehensive employment services run by Aboriginal organizations became available. Employment equity laws that supported an Aboriginal employment network were secured through the Manitoba Civil Service. There have been further gains since the 1980s; however, discrimination in the workplace and cultural barriers continue to exist.

Housing

The lack of decent housing and running water was a critical issue. Housing was a problem in the towns and cities to which Aboriginal women migrated. The IWC worked with emerging housing developments like Kinew Housing under the leadership of Stan Fulham, who was a giant in moving Aboriginal issues through the political systems. Funding was obtained from the Central Mortgage and Housing Corporation to buy fifty homes in Winnipeg for Aboriginal families. The houses were bought in different locations throughout Winnipeg, as not all Aboriginal families lived in the North End neighbourhood of the city. This was an extraordinary time. Single-parent families were provided first opportunities for applying for one of these houses. Single, unemployed mothers benefited as did employed mothers.

Safe Houses and Elder Care

The need for services to care for the elderly was extensive. The Aboriginal elderly in Winnipeg were living in poor housing conditions, and many were living with families, which contributed to overcrowding conditions. Although extended family living is traditional, it added financial worries for the elders as their money did not stretch far enough to adequately feed everyone. Oftentimes they could not afford medicines they required. Although we were not successful in securing medical needs, we were successful in working with the Manitoba Aboriginal Nurses Association to create the Kekinan Centre, a home for elderly Aboriginal citizens. The home provided a safe and warm place for the elders, but they did miss their extended family connections, as family gave companionship and transportation to buy food and for medical visits. Some northern communities were initiating Care Homes for the elders.

Women were being forced to come to the city from outlying communities. Many who lost their treaty status had to leave their communities because they were no longer welcome in their territories. In Winnipeg, there was a definite pressing need for women and children to find safe housing; the women's safe housing in Winnipeg discriminated against Aboriginal women. Osborne House, the only women's shelter in Winnipeg at that time was not a place Aboriginal women felt they could go for protection. The police were not helpful to Aboriginal women in abusive relationships. They frightened Aboriginal women, often accusing them of deserving the abuse they were experiencing. Access to safe houses in towns and in Aboriginal communities has improved since the 1980s; however, Aboriginal women's safety continues to be an issue.

Demonstrations, Political Presentations, and International Representation

Demonstrations: There is a story that made us smile. During one of our demonstrations, as we passed by the courthouse with our loud slogans and colourful banners, one of the judges said, "There goes Peguis First Nation again." But on second look he realized that we were the IWC. His mistake reflects surprise around our organization as well as an appreciation for it. There was also immediate support for our demonstration. We were delighted.

Political presentations: We took our issues to the Senate of Canada, to the provincial and federal governments, and to the United Nations, stating our cases about the violation of our legal, political, social, and economic rights. Of particular concern were the issues of losing treaty status/rights and membership and the right to live in our communities and raise our children with Traditional Knowledge.

International representation: We went to Moscow as Aboriginal women as leaders in our country. When we arrived in Moscow, we were not even on the agenda. We lobbied and made a fuss. We got on the agenda and talked about our issues concerning our treaty and Aboriginal rights. Many women internationally had never heard about the racism that Aboriginal people were facing, and the discriminatory issues facing Aboriginal women.

Justice—Aboriginal Justice Inquiry (AJI)

Helen Betty Osborne, an 18-year-old student from the Norway House First Nation was brutally murdered because she was Aboriginal. She was attending high school in The Pas, Manitoba in the hopes of fulfilling her dream of becoming a teacher. After twenty years of silence, her murder was finally traced to the activities of four men. The town of The Pas and its business establishment protected all four men for all those years. Two were tried: one convicted, one acquitted. One was a witness for the prosecution, and there was not enough evidence to charge the fourth person. Following the trial, the Government of Manitoba appointed an inquiry to investigate the justice system's treatment of Aboriginal people. The IWC was granted standing with the Aboriginal Justice Inquiry due to the case's collective impact and effect on Aboriginal women. Although there was a measure of success in that trial, where guilt was found and punishment assigned, today there are over 1,500 Missing and Murdered Aboriginal Women and Girls, and too many of these cases are still unresolved.[8] At the Helen Betty Osborne Inquiry, a young non-Aboriginal lawyer named Monique Danaher represented the IWC. We are forever grateful to Ms. Danaher for her assistance. During the time when we were working to present our submission to the AJI, I thought about my two small daughters. I was fearful for them and sad and angry about this injustice, and I prayed that they would always be safe and free from racism and harm.

There were other issues about lack of justice, including the fact that so many women were being incarcerated—some for stealing diapers or stealing food and bread because they were financially strapped. These reminded me of Jean Valjean, the hero of Victor Hugo's novel *Les Misérables* who was imprisoned for stealing bread to feed his family, only this was the twentieth century in one of the richest countries in the world! For shame... Public Safety canada[9] indicates that more Aboriginal women are incarcerated today than they were in the 1980s. Portage women's jail was subsequently shut down as recommended by the AJI. Many AJI recommendations have not been implemented by the provincial government.

And Where I Am Now...

Many years have passed since 1985 when Manitoba Aboriginal women created the Indigenous Woman's Collective. The IWC was based on respect, partnership, collaboration, and rooted in Cree values of Whaktowin, Mamawi, Atoskewin, and Dibenimisowin. The organization sparked an energy in us that nourished our hearts and fed our souls with healthy governing energy. The IWC mobilization process was sustained through the power of remembering and utilizing ancestral

8 National Inquiry into Missing and Murdered Indigenous Women and Girls (Canada), *Reclaiming Power and Place: The Final Report of the National Inquiry into Missing and Murdered Indigenous Women and Girls* (Vancouver: Privy Council Office, 2019), https://www.mmiwg-ffada.ca/final-report/.

9 Public Safety Canada, *Marginalized.*

governing knowledge. Leadership was not held by one person; leadership was a shared responsibility and served to strengthen relationships between the various rural and urban Aboriginal women's groups. This bond also served to create respectful and much needed partnerships under a united umbrella with other organizations and the various government agencies. We captured Aboriginal women's strength and power, and I am as certain today as I was then that Aboriginal leadership rooted in our ancestral knowledge of governing can lead us to where we want to go to be healthy and strong.

We had determined that changing leadership every four years would generate strong young leaders that would help to sustain the organization. Each leader would have the opportunity to learn the skills required to lead. That was the ideal. The next leaders were thoughtful young women, who led the organization in their own way. Rural and northern communities were often forgotten in their actions plans. Fragile partnerships and financial resources became an issue. Core funding had provided the initial, necessary start-up support, but regretfully, the IWC lost its ability to hold the organization together. The organization lost its funding, and Manitoba Aboriginal women never regained the strength they needed to bring the IWC back to life.

I think back to that woman who was wearing that bright red dress and how women around her latched on to every word she said, and how I wished that I would someday have her confidence. She was an inspiring woman. I went on to become the president of an organization that had not yet formed. That woman in that red dress always remained in my memory during the years I was president, and whenever I doubted myself, I remembered her and was strengthened by her vitality. She was in many ways my mentor, along with my mother and father who taught me so much about leadership.

Did the organization make a difference in Aboriginal women's lives? I would say that it did. We taught each other that we could make a difference in our lives and in our children's lives by working together and supporting one another. Our children are now all grown up, some with children of their own, so that makes us grandmothers. We created strong networks that still bind us together. There are so many more employed women; daycares are more available; there are many more university graduates who are doctors, nurses, lawyers, professors, administrators, teachers, artists, tradespeople, federal and provincial politicians, Senators. We have gone on to create curriculum that reflects our knowledge, languages, histories, and our cultures. IWC influenced this development. We can all be proud when we reflect back to 1984.

Appendix 1: First Nations and Treaty Areas in Manitoba

Indigenous and Northern Affairs Canada / Affaires autochtones et du Nord Canada

FIRST NATIONS AND TREATY AREAS IN MANITOBA

LEGEND

Non-Aboriginal Communities .... ■

First Nation Communities .... ●

Scale / Échelle 1:3 500 000

Kilometres 0 25 50 100 150 200 Kilomètres

Treaty 1 (1871)

Treaty 2 (1871)

Treaty 3 (1873)

Treaty 4 (1874)

Treaty 5 (1875)

Adhesion to Treaty 5

Explanatory Notes: The boundaries of the Treaty Areas on the map do not correspond in some cases with a Treaty that a First Nation signed. See below.

▲ Fisher River and Kinonjeoshtegon are located in Treaty 2 but are signatory to Treaty 5

◆ Gamblers, Pine Creek, Rolling River, Tootinaowaziibeeng and Waywayseecappo are located in Treaty 2 but signed Treaty 4

◎ Marcel Colomb was formed from Mathias Colomb. Both are located in Treaty 5 adhesion, but signed Treaty 6

☆ Barren Lands and Northlands are located in Treaty 5 adhesion, but signed Treaty 10

○ Peguis is located in Treaty 2 but signed Treaty 1

☒ The Dakota Nations (The Sioux), consisting of Birdtail Sioux, Sioux Valley, Canupawakpa, Dakota Tipi and Dakota Plains are not signatory to any Treaty with Canada

QS-N056-011-EE-A1
Catalogue: R32-270/2017E-PDF
ISBN: 978-0-660-09066-5

Image from Government of Canada website: https://www.sac-isc.gc.ca/eng/1100100020576/1616073943706.

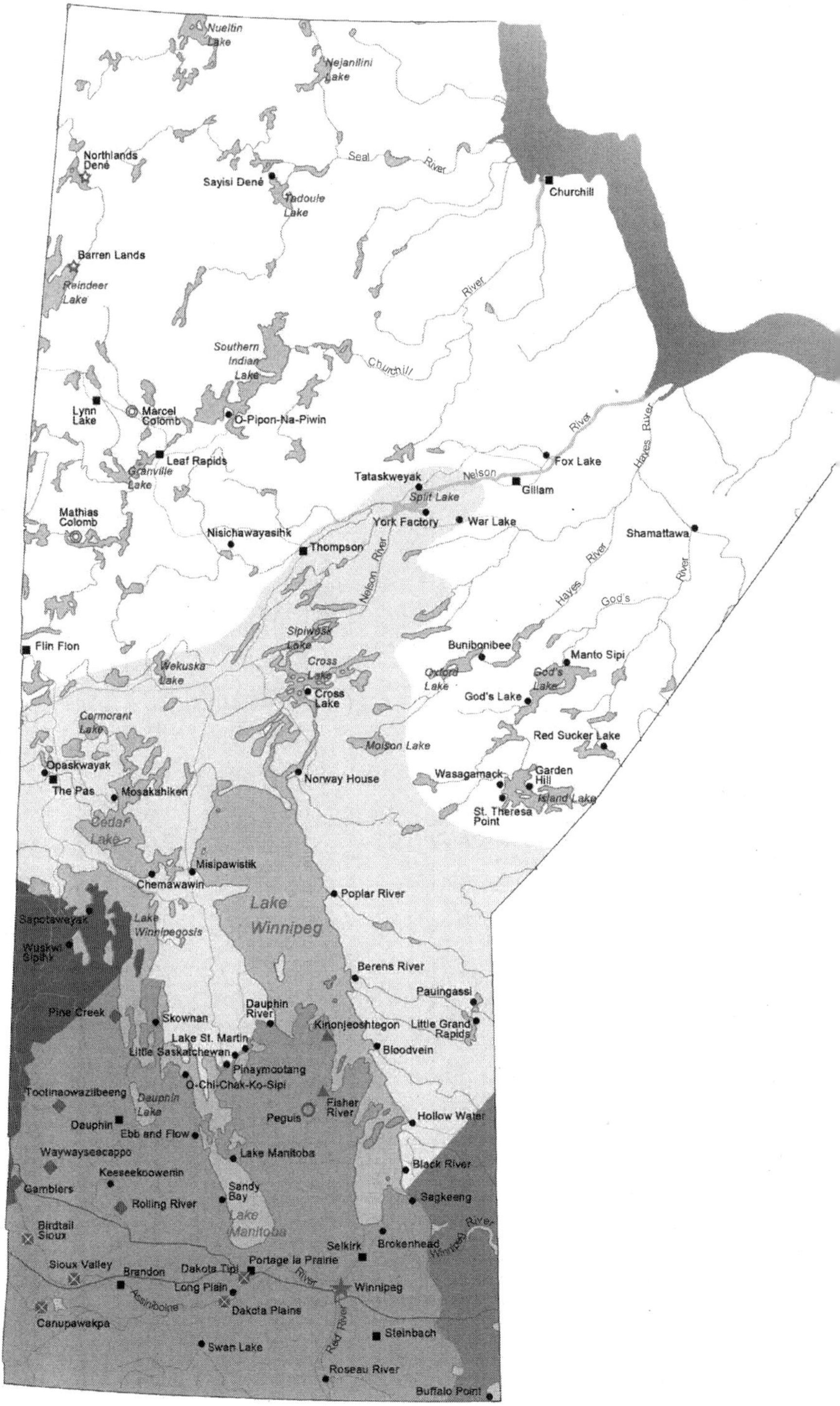

Nueltin Lake
Nejanilini Lake
Northlands Dené
Sayisi Dené
Tadoule Lake
Seal River
Churchill
Barren Lands
Reindeer Lake
Southern Indian Lake
Churchill River
Lynn Lake
Marcel Colomb
O-Pipon-Na-Piwin
Leaf Rapids
Granville Lake
Mathias Colomb
Nisichawayasihk
Thompson
Tataskweyak
Split Lake
Nelson River
York Factory
War Lake
Fox Lake
Gillam
Hayes River
Shamattawa
God's River
Flin Flon
Wekuska Lake
Sipiwesk Lake
Cross Lake
Cross Lake
Bunibonibee
Oxford Lake
Manto Sipi
God's Lake
God's Lake
Red Sucker Lake
Cormorant Lake
Molson Lake
Opaskwayak
The Pas
Mosakahiken
Norway House
Wasagamack
Garden Hill
Island Lake
St. Theresa Point
Cedar Lake
Misipawistik
Chemawawin
Poplar River
Sapotaweyak
Lake Winnipegosis
Lake Winnipeg
Wuskwi Sipihk
Berens River
Pauingassi
Pine Creek
Skownan
Dauphin River
Kinonjeoshtegon
Little Grand Rapids
Lake St. Martin
Little Saskatchewan
Bloodvein
Pinaymootang
O-Chi-Chak-Ko-Sipi
Tootinaowaziibeeng
Dauphin Lake
Dauphin
Peguis
Fisher River
Hollow Water
Ebb and Flow
Waywayseecappo
Lake Manitoba
Black River
Keeseekoowenin
Gamblers
Sandy Bay
Sagkeeng
Rolling River
Lake Manitoba
Birdtail Sioux
Brokenhead
Winnipeg River
Selkirk
Sioux Valley
Brandon
Dakota Tipi
Portage la Prairie
Long Plain
Winnipeg
Assiniboine River
Canupawakpa
Dakota Plains
Red River
Steinbach
Swan Lake
Roseau River
Buffalo Point

Appendix 2: Definitions

1. Aboriginal people are defined in the Constitution Act (1982, Section 35/2) as including First Nation, Inuit, and Métis people of Canada.
2. Non-Status are the Aboriginal people who are neither Treaty nor Métis but identify with their Treaty relatives. Many Non-Status people have tried to reclaim their treaty status. Some have been successful through the passing of Bill C31. Others have to go back in their family records to see what happened to cause them to lose their treaty status. This is sometimes a long and arduous process as church records have been lost or destroyed, or their births were never registered.

Bibliography

Betasamosake Simpson, Leanne. *As We Have Always Done: Indigenous Freedom through Radical Resistance.* Minneapolis and London: University of Minnesota Press, 2017.

Brennan, Frank, and Miriam Rose Ungunmerr-Baumann. "Reverencing the Earth in the Australian Dreaming." *The Way* 29, 1 (1989): 38–45.

Kimelman, Judge E.C. *No Quiet Place: Review Committee on Indian and Métis Adoption and Placements.* Winnipeg: Manitoba Department of Community Service and Corrections, 1985.

Loxley, John, Bernie Wood, Louise Champagne, E.J. Fontaine, and Charles Scribe. *Aboriginal People in the Winnipeg Economy: Case Study.* Royal Commission on Aboriginal Peoples, Ottawa, Volume 5, 1996.

Manitoba Aboriginal Justice Inquiry, A.C. Hamilton, and C. M Sinclair. *Report of the Aboriginal Justice Inquiry of Manitoba.* Volume II: The Death of Helen Betty Osborne. Manitoba: Province of Manitoba, 1991. http://www.ajic.mb.ca/volumell/toc.html.

National Indian Brotherhood/Assembly of First Nations, *Indian Control of Indian Education*, policy paper presented to the Minister of Indian Affairs and Northern Development, Ottawa: National Indian Brotherhood/Assembly of First Nations, 1972. https://oneca.com/IndianControlofIndianEducation.pdf.

National Inquiry into Missing and Murdered Indigenous Women and Girls (Canada). *Reclaiming Power and Place: The Final Report of the National Inquiry into Missing and Murdered Indigenous Women and Girls.* Vancouver: Privy Council Office, 2019. https://www.mmiwg-ffada.ca/final-report/.

Public Safety Canada. *Marginalized: The Aboriginal Women's Experience in Federal Corrections.* Ottawa: Public Safety Canada, 2012.

The Truth and Reconciliation Commission of Canada. *Honouring the Truth, Reconciling for the Future.* Summary of the Final Report of the Truth and Reconciliation Commission of Canada, 2015. https://www.sac-isc.gc.ca/eng/1100100020576/1616073943706.

Wagamese, Richard. *Embers: One Ojibway's Meditations.* Madeira Park, BC: Douglas and McIntyre, 2016.

Chapter 7

Indigenous Resistance and Development in Child Welfare:

The Story of Ma Mawi Wi Chi Itata Centre

Shauna MacKinnon and Kathy Mallett

> "We are saying in a strong unified manner: We are no longer going to be controlled by the Board of Children's Aid"[1]—Member of the Coalition on Native Child Welfare

In 1984, Indigenous people in Winnipeg created the Ma Mawi Wi Chi Itata Centre, an Indigenous-led social service agency. Their goal was to provide services to Indigenous children and families in need and to ultimately ensure that children remained with their families. Vern Morrissette, a member of Ma Mawi Wi Chi Itata Centre board in 1984 and first board president, describes the centre as having "been born from the ashes of a failed child welfare system that acted as one of the many agents toward cultural genocide and the dismantling of Aboriginal family life."[2] In this chapter, we describe a complex and

1 Canadian Broadcasting Corporation, footage from 1982. CAN 432 and 436. 13:25, Archives of Manitoba.

2 Vern Morrissette, *A Document Respecting Culture, Traditions and The Historical Experiences of Aboriginal People on the Operations of the Centre* (Winnipeg: Aboriginal Perspectives, n.d.), 1.

interconnected series of events, policies, and crises that culminated in frustration, anger, mobilization, and in the eventual creation of Ma Mawi Wi Chi Itata Centre. Although the efforts of Indigenous activists did not ultimately fix a broken system, it was an important step in the ongoing fight to reclaim Indigenous control over child welfare.

Activists involved in the creation of Ma Mawi Wi Chi Itata Centre were responding to non-Indigenous child welfare agencies apprehending Indigenous children and placing them in non-Indigenous families where the children failed to thrive and all too often lost contact with the Indigenous community. The creation of Ma Mawi Wi Chi Itata Centre is part of a broader re-assertion of Indigenous rights to self-government that can be traced back at least to the the policy paper, Indian Control of Indian Education, presented to the federal government in 1972.[3]

Indigenous entanglement in the child welfare system must be viewed in a historical context of colonial policies that align with cultural genocide.[4] Multiple government and independent inquiries, reports, and commissions over many years have exposed the negative intentions and consequences of colonialist child welfare policies in Canada. Government responses have been slow and inadequate at best. From Confederation onwards, the Canadian government's policy toward Indigenous families and children has been part of a broader policy intended to end the government's treaty obligations to First Nations. Under the residential school policy, children were to be taken from their parents, educated in a new religion and new language, with

3 National Indian Brotherhood/Assembly of First Nations, *Indian Control of Indian Education*, policy paper presented to the Minister of Indian Affairs and Northern Development (Ottawa: National Indian Brotherhood/Assembly of First Nations, 1972), https://oneca.com/IndianControlofIndianEducation.pdf.

4 The Truth and Reconciliation Commission (TRC) of Canada, *Canada's Residential Schools: The History, Part 1, Origins to 1939, The Final Report of the Truth and Reconciliation Commission of Canada, Volume I* (Winnipeg: The Truth and Reconciliation Commission of Canada, 2015).

the expectation that they would not return to their home community and would give up their legal rights as First Nations people. When Duncan Campbell Scott said in 1920 that Canada's "objective is to continue until there is not a single Indian in Canada that has not been absorbed into the body politic," he was speaking about a bill that would give the government the right to compel children to attend residential school. Once there were no "Indians," there would be no reserves and no treaty obligations.[5]

The residential schools failed to achieve their intended goals, but they did wreak havoc on Indigenous children, families, and communities. The schools were poorly built, poorly funded, and poorly maintained. Death rates were high, punishment harsh, education inadequate, and the risk of sexual abuse was significant. A notable legacy of the schools is the disruption of Indigenous traditions of parenting, including the role of the extended family.

The evident failure of the residential schools led the federal government to begin to transfer responsibility for Indigenous child welfare to provincial governments in 1951. (The process of closing the schools was a slow one that was not completed until the 1990s.) But the practice of transferring power to provincial governments proved to be similarly disastrous for Indigenous people.[6]

Provincial governments had long been involved in child welfare dating back to the late 1800s when they began to fund private non-profit children's aid societies. These agencies were initially established in urban areas to respond to the negative impact that industrialization and urbanization had on low-income families. Poor housing, limited sanitation, dangerous working conditions, and limited incomes meant that the children of many working-class families came to be seen as being in need of rescue. Children's aid societies were mandated by

5 Ibid.

6 See The Truth and Reconciliation Commission, *Canada's Residential Schools: The History, Part 1*; and The Truth and Reconciliation Commission, *Canada's Residential Schools: The History, Part 2*.

provincial governments to take children into custody and place them with foster or adoptive parents when they determined children were at risk of neglect or abuse; notably, they based their determinations on the dominant culture's norms.[7]

Children's aid societies generally had limited geographic borders: take for example the Children's Aid Society of Winnipeg (CASW) or the Children's Aid Society of Southwestern Manitoba. In theory, the separation of children from their parents has always been only one of the tools in the child welfare toolkit. Interventions have always included a range of preventive options intended to address child welfare problems while maintaining family unity. However, for Indigenous families involved with Children's Aid Societies, apprehension became the primary tool of choice.

Starting in the 1950s, First Nations families increasingly began migrating from rural and northern Manitoba to the city of Winnipeg. There they found themselves experiencing challenges similar to other families on the bottom of the economic and social ladder. They also experienced a form of racism that was deeply systemic. Employment opportunities were limited, housing was expensive, and families were

7 John Bullen, "J.J. Kelso and the New Child-Savers: The Genesis of the Children's Aid Movement in Ontario," in *Dimensions of Childhood: Essays on the History of Children and Youth in Canada,* ed. R. Smandych, G. Dodds, and A. Esau, 135–158 (Manitoba: Legal Research Institute, 1991); Bettina Bradbury, "The Fragmented Family: Family Strategies in the Face of Death, Illness, and Poverty, Montreal, 1860–1885," in *Childhood and Family in Canadian History,* ed. Joy Parr, 109–128 (Toronto: McClelland and Stewart, 1982); Cynthia Comacchio, *Nations are Built of Babies: Saving Ontario's Mothers and Children, 1900–1940* (Montreal: McGill-Queen's University Press, 1993); Len Kaminski, "Laura Crouch and The Home of the Friendless," *Manitoba History* 80 (Spring 2016): 37–46; Neil Sutherland and Cynthia Comacchio, *Children in English-Canadian Society: Framing the Twentieth-Century Consensus* (Waterloo: Wilfrid Laurier University Press, 2006); Aleda Turnbull, "Progressive Social Policy in Manitoba, 1915–1939," (Master's Thesis, University of Manitoba, 1980); Jane Ursel, *Private Lives, Public Policy: 100 Years of State Intervention in the Family* (Toronto: Women's Press, 1992).

struggling with the legacy of residential schooling. That legacy is one of intergenerational trauma. Residential school survivors were commonly neglected and abused. They were torn from their families and cultures and placed in institutions where they did not receive love and parenting. Many suffered from multiple forms of abuse. As adults, survivors struggled to cope with the trauma. Having not been parented themselves, many struggled as parents. The response from the child welfare system emulated residential school policy. Instead of addressing the cause by offering parents a range of supports, children deemed to be at risk were swiftly removed from their families and placed in non-Indigenous homes.

This is the tragic story of what has come to be known as the Sixties Scoop (although it should be noted that the practice continued long after the decade of the 1960s ended). In a 1983 critique of the child welfare system, Patrick Johnston introduced the term Sixties Scoop to describe the dramatic increase in the number of Indigenous children apprehended from their families and placed in the care of the state. Johnston describes interviewing a remorseful retired social worker who recalled the ill-intended policy and practice where she and her colleagues "scooped" children from reserves "almost as a matter of course."[8] In his 1985 report on the Manitoba Child Welfare system *No Quiet Place*, Associate Chief Justice Edwin Kimelman describes the impact of this practice: "Children who entered the system were generally lost to family and community—or were returned with there having been little input to change the situation from which they were taken in the first place."[9]

Appointed by the Province of Manitoba in 1982 to examine concerns raised by Indigenous leaders regarding the placement of

8 Patrick Johnston, "Revisiting the 'Sixties Scoop' of Indigenous Children," *Policy Options*, July 26, 2016. https://policyoptions.irpp.org/magazines/july-2016/revisiting-the-sixties-scoop-of-indigenous-children/.

9 Judge E.C. Kimelman, *No Quiet Place: Review Committee on Indian and Métis Adoption and Placements* (Winnipeg: Manitoba Department of Community Service and Corrections, 1985), 273.

Indigenous children in non-Indigenous homes outside of the province, Justice Kimelman reviewed the file of "every Native child who had been adopted by an out-of-province family in 1981." He concluded "unequivocally that cultural genocide has been taking place in a systematic, routine manner."[10] He called for a transformation of the child welfare system and presented 109 recommendations for change.

Although there have been some improvements in Manitoba's child welfare system since the Kimelman report was released, Indigenous children continue to be apprehended from their families at an alarming rate. The Kimelman report would not be the last to reveal a deeply flawed system that has failed Indigenous children and families. The Aboriginal Justice Inquiry (1991) heard repeatedly of systemic problems in child welfare. Many years later, the Inquiry into the Circumstances Surrounding the Death of Phoenix Sinclair revealed many of the same issues, including the continued overrepresentation of Indigenous children in the child welfare system and insufficient provision of resources for prevention.[11]

While the safety of children sometimes requires that they be taken into care, these reports have shown that removing Indigenous children from their families and communities can also have a tragic impact. Indigenous children in care are all too often bounced from foster home to foster home and often from school to school, impeding the development of relationships with family, peers, caregivers, and teachers. Facing racism at every turn, children in care learn to distrust at a very young age. Some drop out of school. Some turn to street gangs. Some make choices that, while harmful, make sense to them as they seek a sense of belonging and escape from the pain of childhoods lost. While many survive and break free, far too many do not, and the cycle continues.

10 Ibid., 272.

11 Inquiry into the Circumstances Surrounding the Death of Phoenix Sinclair, 2014. http://www.phoenixsinclairinquiry.ca

Indigenous-Led Resistance

This cycle closely resembled the experience many Indigenous activists in the 1970s and '80s knew about residential schools. They saw that both residential school and child welfare policies were rooted in the same colonial aspirations—to strip Indigenous children from their families, communities, and cultures. It was clear that the closure of residential schools, which commenced in earnest in 1970, was accompanied by a significant increase in the number of children being taken into care by child welfare agencies. The intent seemed clear. Kimelman revealed

> an abysmal lack of sensitivity... Families approached agencies for help and found that what was described as being in the child's "best interest" resulted in their families being torn asunder and siblings separated. Social workers grappled with cultural patterns far different from their own with no preparation and no opportunities to gain understanding.[12]

Control of child welfare had long been central to Indigenous leaders' assertion of their rights to self-government. The continued exclusion of Indigenous leadership in developing and implementing policies pertaining to child welfare was increasingly apparent. It was clear that in the name of "protection," the child welfare practices of the provincial government closely resembled residential school policies.

Indigenous leaders called for an end to the apprehension of Indigenous children, demanding full control over Indigenous child welfare. By the late 1970s, the Government of Manitoba began to respond. In 1977, it established the Indian Child Welfare Sub-Committee, which consisted of representatives from two provincial government departments, two federal government departments, and the Manitoba Indian Brotherhood, which represented 49 First Nations. The work of the committee was completed in 1980, and its final report made several

12 Kimelman, 174.

recommendations. It identified the importance of preserving "Indian identity," including language and culture, and called for Indigenous peoples to be involved in the development of their own services.[13]

Although there were a number of Indigenous-run child welfare agencies established in Manitoba (outside of Winnipeg) in the late 1970s and early 1980s, Indigenous leaders remained highly critical of the system. Although the government had decided to establish First Nation–led regional child welfare agencies in response to Indigenous calls for action, the mandates of the agencies would continue to fall under provincial legislation. Many Indigenous leaders were suspicious of the government's intent and continued to argue that anything short of self-governance over child and family services was unacceptable.[14]

First Nation agencies generally served children and families in First Nations, not in urban centres. Indigenous children and families in Winnipeg continued to fall under the jurisdiction of the non-Indigenous CASW. Indigenous child welfare activists were increasingly convinced that this needed to change. The impetus to mobilize was sparked by the tragic death of an 18-month-old Indigenous child while in the care of CASW in May 1982. As reported by the *Winnipeg Free Press,* the child was found dead "following a bathtub mishap in which the child was found under water."[15] The parents were reportedly not informed until twenty-four hours after the incident occurred.

Outraged and more determined than ever to reclaim control over child welfare matters, activists stepped up their organizing efforts and formed the Winnipeg Coalition on Native Child Welfare. The Coalition was mainly driven by women, including Louise Champagne,

13 Manitoba Aboriginal Justice Inquiry, A.C. Hamilton, and C. M Sinclair, *Report of the Aboriginal Justice Inquiry of Manitoba,* Volume I: The Justice System and Aboriginal People (Winnipeg: Aboriginal Justice Inquiry of Manitoba, 1991), 521.

14 Ibid, 523.

15 Cecil Rosner, "CAS Ward Dead Following Tub Mishap," *Winnipeg Free Press,* May 10, 1982.

Linda Clarkson, Kathy Mallett, and many others.[16] Its mission was to reclaim control over Indigenous child welfare. The coalition identified four priorities:

1. To lobby for the establishment of a fully mandated native child welfare agency. (Mandated child welfare agencies have legal authority to apprehend children.)
2. To lobby for the establishment of a (non-mandated) Native child and family support agency. (Non-mandated agencies do not have legal authority to apprehend.)
3. To lobby for reforms to the existing system.
4. To strengthen the Coalition through acquisition of staff.

Coalition members immediately advocated for seats on the CASW Board. They demanded half of the thirty-two seats; they were offered seven. In May 1982, the same month as the tragic death of the child in the care of CASW, the Coalition chartered a bus and transported Indigenous families to the CASW annual general meeting where they would publicly decline the offer and make their intentions known. Coalition spokeswomen Myrna Whitehawk and Yvonne House addressed the board and those in attendance, which included over 200 Indigenous supporters, informing them that that they were no longer willing to support CASW's authority over their children. They were firm in their assertion: "We are no longer going to accept their model of service delivery that is apprehension, not prevention. We no longer recognize CAS as a child protection agency. Our children are dying."[17]

16 Activists refer to the Coalition as the Winnipeg Coalition on Native Child Welfare. The AJI report refers to it as the Winnipeg Urban Indian Coalition. See the Manitoba Aboriginal Justice Inquiry, Hamilton, and Sinclair, *Report of the Aboriginal Justice Inquiry*, 529.

17 Canada Broadcasting Corporation, footage from 1982. Archives of Manitoba. CAN 432 and 436. 13:25.

After denouncing the policies and practices of the CASW, they presented a petition to the provincial government demanding it mandate an Indigenous-led agency to deliver child welfare services to Indigenous people in Winnipeg. The petition was denied. The Coalition continued its campaign for an Indigenous-run centre in Winnipeg where Indigenous child-caring values and beliefs would guide service to families. This activism contributed to increased pressure on the provincial government to act, and a series of events occurred during this period that eventually led to the establishment of Ma Mawi Wi Chi Itata Centre.

That year, the province ordered a stop to adoptions out of province and appointed Justice Kimelman to lead an inquiry to fully examine the child welfare system related to Indigenous children and families. Prior to the release of the Kimelman report, which called for a major overhaul of the child welfare system, the province began phasing out the CASW, and in 1985, the centralized model was replaced with six regional-based agencies. The intention behind the objective aligned with Kimelman's recommendation to "make service more sensitive of the cultural patterns of neighbourhoods and with the full participation of the residents of the communities by having these residents sit on the various boards as directors."[18] As a compromise to the call for an Indigenous child welfare agency in Winnipeg, the province proposed a majority of Indigenous people be appointed to the board of the Child and Family Services of Central Winnipeg. Failing to agree on structure and representation, the Coalition chose to return to its original plan to establish an Indigenous child welfare agency.

In March 1984, a working group—including the Coalition, Native Family Services, the School of Social Work, and the Province of Manitoba—finalized a proposal for a Native Child and Family Support Centre. Vern Morrissette describes the proposed centre as a non-mandated agency operating independently, in conjunction with the regional agencies. The agency would provide "community development,

18 Kimelman, *No Quiet Place*, 276.

support to families at risk or in crisis, advocacy for children in care and other services," steeped in Indigenous cultures and traditions.[19]

Not everyone agreed with the proposal. Some wanted an agency with all of the powers of a mandated agency, which included the responsibility to apprehend children it determined to be in need of protection according to the provincial Child and Family Services Act. Other proponents argued that a mandated agency would be bound by provincial legislation, thereby requiring compliance with the very oppressive colonial policies that they opposed. Others fell somewhere in the middle, believing that they should accept the province's offer and continue their advocacy for greater control. In the end, the Coalition accepted $1 million for operations and made clear its position that the establishment of the non-mandated agency did not replace negotiations for a mandated Indigenous child welfare agency. The Coalition established an election committee and process. Two hundred eighteen members of the Indigenous community elected a twelve-member board of Directors and Ma Mawi Wi Chi Itata Centre, Inc. was born.

Ma Mawi Wi Chi Itata Centre: We All Work Together to Help One Another

In 1984, the Ma Mawi Wi Chi Itata Centre opened its doors in a small office on Selkirk Avenue. It received funding from the Manitoba government to provide supports to Indigenous families in need and to prevent children from being taken into foster care. Its central mission was to "develop a model of service" built from the premise of "Aboriginal people serving Aboriginal people" that emphasized prevention and support.[20] It did not have a mandate to apprehend children.

The story of Ma Mawi Wi Chi Itata Centre, now celebrating over thirty-six years of services, is an important chapter in the history of

19 Larry Morrissette, "The Ma Mawi Wi Chi Itata Centre, Inc.," in *Protecting our Children: National American Indian Conference on Child Abuse and Neglect* (Albuquerque: American Indian Institute; University of Oklahoma, 1988).

20 Vern Morrissette, *A Document Respecting Culture*, 17.

child and family services for Indigenous families in Manitoba. It is also an important story of grassroots organizing—an example of local Indigenous resistance to settler colonial genocide on Turtle Island, and an "amazing example of activism ... the catalyst" for future Indigenous development initiatives.[21]

Although Ma Mawi Wi Chi Itata Centre continues to be a strong voice for Indigenous families in Winnipeg, there have been challenges along the way. In a 2013 interview, Vern Morrissette, one of the founding members of Ma Mawi Wi Chi Itata Centre, describes some critical discussions that took place throughout the years as the urban Indigenous community "developed an analysis and response to colonialism." Not everyone always agreed, and this led to a "schism" between those who wanted to "continue on a traditional path to developing a service model" compared with those who thought a better approach was to "penetrate mainstream service systems, take over mainstream institutions ... just become those mainstream institutions."[22] Morrissette describes a central question debated by Indigenous child welfare activists at the time: "Do we just attach brown faces to white institutions? People may think that is a harsh analysis, but it is not. It is really what was going on, and some ways it continues to happen today."

For Morrissette, the answer was clear. He believed it was important that Ma Mawi Wi Chi Itata Centre remain true to its roots:

> For me, the most important lesson that I have learned is that we stand on the shoulders of our ancestors. We are here because of those people who came before us ... who [would not] give up who they were, who fought tooth and nail to maintain their identities. I'll be damned if I will give that away ... That was the fight of the women in the coalition. They fought to maintain their identity—who they were as Aboriginal women ... We are still trying to figure out how to be true to our identity.

21 Vern Morrissette, interview by Darrell Chippeway and Larry Morrissette, 2013.

22 Vern Morrissette, interview.

The debate continued and for a time in the 1990s, Ma Mawi Wi Chi Itata Centre was criticized for moving away from its community roots. Having relocated its head office to Broadway Avenue as a temporary measure, and after an unresolved health and safety concern at the Aboriginal Centre of Winnipeg, "the Ma Mawi Wi Chi Itata Centre turned inward for a time, attempting to resolve their inner turmoil, confusion, and the split in the community."[23] As a result, there was a concern that the organization had become overly bureaucratic and distant from the community. Vern Morrissette notes that "there is some sense of truth to this concern, but it's easy to oversimplify the political turmoil and its effects on the Ma Mawi Wi Chi Itata staff." Although the new Aboriginal Centre of Winnipeg brought promise, it came with ambivalence and uncertainty about Ma Mawi Wi Chi Itata Centre's continued role in growing the resources for the community beyond child welfare. As past director Josie Hill describes, "most people didn't even know Ma Mawi Wi Chi Itata existed."[24] However, consultations with the Indigenous community brought Ma Mawi Wi Chi Itata Centre back to its roots, and under Hill's direction, Ma Mawi Wi Chi Itata Centre re-established its focus on community. It relocated its head office to McGregor Avenue in the North End and continued to offer community-driven child and family services from various community locations.

In 2009, the Manitoba Public Insurance Corporation closed its 445 King Street claim centre and donated the building to Ma Mawi Wi Chi Itata Centre, where it continues to offer a number of services to families. This location has firmly rooted Ma Mawi Wi Chi Itata in the North End, close to its first home on Selkirk Avenue. In addition to offering various programs, including Indigenous ceremonies, community training, and youth programming, the 445 King Street location has become Winnipeg's Gathering Place for Truth and Reconciliation. Ma Mawi Wi Chi Itata Centre continues to be a non-mandated agency without powers to apprehend children. It is led by a community board,

23 Vern Morrissette, personal communication, 17 August, 2021.

24 Jim Silver, *In Their Own Voices*, 154).

and it remains closely connected with the community it serves. Ma Mawi Wi Chi Itata Centre continues to integrate Indigenous knowledge and traditions into its many programs, including parent support programs, family reunification programs, youth programming, addiction supports, and Head Start early learning programs. Ma Mawi Wi Chi Itata Centre describes its many programs as helping families plan for the future while also providing emergency supports for those living in poverty. Importantly, almost everyone who works at Ma Mawi Wi Chi Itata is Indigenous and can therefore personally relate to the experiences that have led families to need their support. Indigenous families trust that Ma Mawi Wi Chi Itata Centre understands their challenges and will help them stay together.

Ma Mawi Wi Chi Itata Centre's operating budget has grown significantly since 1984. Its initial annual budget of $1 million has grown to $22 million. Some 250 Indigenous staff and 800 volunteers provide service to over 30,000 families annually, through more than fifty programs at sixteen sites. Many of the individuals who initially reached out to Ma Mawi Wi Chi Itata Centre for support continue to be involved as volunteers and mentors to other families. This is a testament to the value that Ma Mawi Wi Chi Itata Centre places on community strength, mutual respect, and reciprocity.

In addition to providing a number of services to families, Ma Mawi Wi Chi Itata Centre continues to advocate for systemic changes in child welfare and other policies that impact Indigenous families. The centre continues to operate from the philosophy that the challenges families face are primarily systemic, and it remains focused on its decolonizing aims to "discard Western practices designed to assimilate aboriginal peoples."[25] Ma Mawi Wi Chi Itata Centre recognizes that the legacy of residential schools and the Sixties Scoop continues to affect multiple generations of Indigenous families. So, while the model of service continues to evolve, with new programs developed

25 Vern Morrissette, *A Document Respecting Culture*, 19.

to meet evolving needs, Ma Mawi Wi Chi Itata Centre's leadership continues to be informed from an understanding of the historical context of colonialism.[26]

In the 1991 *Report of the Aboriginal Justice Inquiry*, Justice Alvin Hamilton and Judge Murray Sinclair describes the Ma Mawi Wi Chi Itata Centre's Aboriginal approach to child welfare as "serving the interests of the child best by ensuring a supportive family or, failing that, a supportive extended family [that] encompasses the whole community."[27] Among their many recommendations, they called for continued support for Ma Mawi Wi Chi Itata Centre, emphasizing that it should "remain a non-mandated agency."[28] Ma Mawi Chi Ita Centre's sustainability over many years is a testament to the centre's commitment to Indigenous-led child and family services. But its growth reflects the troubling reality that many of the challenges identified by Indigenous leaders forty-some years ago have yet to be addressed.

Indigenous Child Welfare Beyond 2020: Implications for Ma Mawi Wi Chi Itata Centre

While some things have changed since 1984, much has not. After the Aboriginal Justice Inquiry report was shelved for ten years by a Conservative government in the 1990s, some of its recommendations were implemented by a New Democratic Party government through the Aboriginal Justice Inquiry – Child Welfare Initiative. In Manitoba, under the Child and Family Services (CFS) division and four CFS authorities, there are twenty-seven CFS agencies and regional offices that work together to deliver child and family services throughout the province in accordance with The Child and Family Services Act, The Adoption Act, and The Child and Family Services Authorities Act. Three of the four authorities—the First Nations of Northern Manitoba

26 Ibid., 22.

27 Manitoba Aboriginal Justice Inquiry, Hamilton, and Sinclair, *Report of the Aboriginal Justice Inquiry*, 529–530.

28 Ibid, 529.

CFS Authority (Northern Authority), the Southern First Nations Network of Care (Southern Network), and the Métis CFS Authority—are responsible for providing support to nineteen Indigenous CFS agencies across the province. This model of governance is unique to Manitoba. While it has moved the needle on Indigenous governance over child welfare, it remains the case that Indigenous child welfare agencies are bound by provincial legislation. And there continues to be an overwhelming number of Indigenous children in foster care. In Manitoba, there are now more than 10,000 children in care and upwards of ninety percent of these children are Indigenous.[29]

This is a stark reminder that many of the root causes highlighted in *No Quiet Place* (1984) and the *Report of the Aboriginal Justice Inquiry of Manitoba* (1991) persist, as described more recently in the *Legacy of Phoenix Sinclair: Achieving the Best for All Our Children Inquiry into the Death of Phoenix Sinclair* (2013), by the Truth and Reconciliation Commission (2015), and in *Reclaiming Power and Place: The Final Report of the National Inquiry into Missing and Murdered Indigenous Women and Girls* (2019).[30] As was the case before Ma Mawi Wi Chi Itata Centre opened its doors, far too many Indigenous families

29 Government of Manitoba Department of Families, *Annual Report 2019–20* (Winnipeg: Manitoba Families, 2020), https://www.gov.mb.ca/fs/about/pubs/fsar_2019-2020.pdf.

30 Kimelman, *No Quiet Place*; Manitoba Aboriginal Justice Inquiry, Hamilton, and Sinclair, *Report of the Aboriginal Justice Inquiry*; Ted Hughes, *The Legacy of Phoenix Sinclair: Achieving the Best for All Our Children*, Volumes I and II (Winnipeg: Commission of Inquiry into the Circumstances Surrounding the Death of Phoenix Sinclair, 2013); The Truth and Reconciliation Commission (TRC) of Canada, *Honouring the Truth, Reconciling for the Future Summary of the Final Report of the Truth and Reconciliation Commission of Canada* (Winnipeg: The Truth and Reconciliation Commission of Canada, 2015); National Inquiry into Missing and Murdered Indigenous Women and Girls (Canada), *Reclaiming Power and Place: The Final Report of the National Inquiry into Missing and Murdered Indigenous Women and Girls* (Vancouver: Privy Council Office, 2019). https://www.mmiwg-ffada.ca/final-report/.

continue to live in poverty, many suffer from the intergenerational trauma of residential schools and the Sixties Scoop, and systemic racism persists.

Within this context, Indigenous people continue to fight for sovereignty over the care, protection, and nurturance of their children. Child welfare policy continues to be provincially and territorially funded and legislated, with the exception of federally funded services to First Nations peoples living on reserves. A new federal act, An Act Respecting First Nations, Inuit and Métis Children, Youth and Families, came into effect January 1, 2020. Aligned with what Ma Mawi Wi Chi Itata Centre has always hoped to achieve, this act reinforces Indigenous sovereignty over child welfare. The act includes new national standards and three core principles—the best interest of the child, cultural continuity, and substantive equality. The act is "the first federal legislation on the subject of Indigenous child and family services and the first statute to recognize inherent Indigenous jurisdiction over child and family services as a Section 35 right in Canada."[31] Important for Ma Mawi Wi Chi Itata Centre is that the federal act stresses the importance of culture and family beyond what is currently in Manitoba's child welfare legislation. The act has the potential to ensure agencies like Ma Mawi Wi Chi Itata Centre are better funded to provide culturally-based services to strengthen families and reduce the number of Indigenous children taken into care.

The 2018 report from Manitoba's Legislative Review Committee *Transforming Child Welfare Legislation in Manitoba: Opportunities to Improve Outcomes for Children and Youth* outlines a number of changes that, if implemented, would improve the system. But it also clearly states that these are interim measures and that "the committee's long-term goal for child welfare reform is to create legislation that enables Indigenous peoples to have their own child welfare system

31 Friedland, Hadley, *Bill C-92 National Standards Guide for Legal Professionals* (Wahkohtowin Law and Governance Lodge, 2020), 1.

that respects their right to self-determination."[32] This review is yet one more report strengthening the case for Indigenous sovereignty over child welfare, the guiding principle central to the Ma Mawi Wi Chi Itata Centre's story.

Ma Mawi Wi Chi Itata is an important example of Indigenous resistance and development in Winnipeg. The centre has been an important resource for Indigenous families for over thirty-six years. It has also been a respected and consistent voice calling for greater Indigenous control over policies and programs serving Indigenous children and families, and it has served as a "catalyst that started everything in the community" (see Chapter 6).[33]

There has been progress, but it has been slow, and many challenges remain. Self-governance over child welfare has yet to be achieved, and far too many Indigenous children continue to be placed into foster care. Ma Mawi Wi Chi Itata's leadership continues to advocate for meaningful systemic change to redress continued issues and to reclaim Indigenous sovereignty over Indigenous child welfare.

Bibliography

Bradbury, Bettina. "The Fragmented Family: Family Strategies in the Face of Death, Illness, and Poverty, Montreal, 1860–1885." In *Childhood and Family in Canadian History*, edited by Joy Parr, 109–128. Toronto: McClelland and Stewart, 1982.

Bullen, John. "J.J. Kelso and the New Child-Savers: The Genesis of the Children's Aid Movement in Ontario." In *Dimensions of Childhood: Essays on the History of Children and Youth in Canada*, edited by R. Smandych, G. Dodds, and A. Esau, 135–158. Manitoba: Legal Research Institute, 1991.

32 Government of Manitoba, *Transforming Child Welfare Legislation in Manitoba: Opportunities to Improve Outcomes for Children and Youth Report of the Legislative Review Committee* (Winnipeg: Government of Manitoba, 2018), 28.

33 Vern Morrissette, interview.

Canadian Broadcasting Corporation. Footage from 1982. Archives of Manitoba. CAN 432 and 436. 13:25.

Comacchio, Cynthia. *Nations are Built of Babies: Saving Ontario's Mothers and Children, 1900–1940*. Montreal: McGill-Queen's University Press, 1993.

Friedland, Hadley. *Bill C-92 National Standards Guide for Legal Professionals*. Wahkohtowin Law and Governance Lodge, 2020.

Government of Manitoba. *Transforming Child Welfare Legislation in Manitoba: Opportunities to Improve Outcomes for Children and Youth Report of the Legislative Review Committee*. Winnipeg: Government of Manitoba, 2018.

Government of Manitoba Department of Families. *Annual Report 2019–20*. Winnipeg: Manitoba Families, 2020. https://www.gov.mb.ca/fs/about/pubs/fsar_2019-2020.pdf.

Hughes, Ted. *The Legacy of Phoenix Sinclair: Achieving the Best for All Our Children.* Volumes I and II. Winnipeg: Commission of the Inquiry into the Circumstances Surrounding the Death of Phoenix Sinclair, 2013.

Johnston, Patrick. "Revisiting the 'Sixties Scoop' of Indigenous Children." *Policy Options*, July 26, 2016. https://policyoptions.irpp.org/magazines/july-2016/revisiting-the-sixties-scoop-of-indigenous-children/.

Kaminski, Len. "Laura Crouch and The Home of the Friendless." *Manitoba History* 80 (Spring 2016): 37–46.

Kimelman, Judge E.C. *No Quiet Place: Review Committee on Indian and Métis Adoption and Placements*. Winnipeg: Manitoba Department of Community Service and Corrections, 1985.

Manitoba Aboriginal Justice Inquiry, A.C. Hamilton, and C. M Sinclair. *Report of the Aboriginal Justice Inquiry of Manitoba*. Volume I: The Justice System and Aboriginal People. Winnipeg: Aboriginal Justice Inquiry of Manitoba, 1991.

Morrissette, Larry. "The Ma Mawi Wi Chi Itata Centre, Inc." In *Protecting our Children: National American Indian Conference on Child Abuse and Neglect.* Albuquerque: American Indian Institute; University of Oklahoma, 1988.

Morrissette, Vern. *A Document Respecting Culture, Traditions and The Historical Experiences of Aboriginal People on the Operations of the Centre.* Winnipeg: Aboriginal Perspectives, n.d.

Morrissette, Vern. Interview by Darrell Chippeway and Larry Morrissette, 2013.

Morrissette, Vern. Personal communication. 17 August 2021.

National Indian Brotherhood/Assembly of First Nations. *Indian Control of Indian Education.* Policy paper presented to the Minister of Indian Affairs and Northern Development. Ottawa: National Indian Brotherhood/Assembly of First Nations, 1972. https://oneca.com/IndianControlofIndianEducation.pdf.

Rosner, Cecil. "CAS Ward Dead Following Tub Mishap." *Winnipeg Free Press,* May 10, 1982.

Silver, Jim. *In Their Own Voices: Building Urban Aboriginal Communities.* Winnipeg: Fernwood, 2006.

Sutherland, Neil, and Cynthia Comacchio. *Children in English-Canadian Society: Framing the Twentieth-Century Consensus.* Waterloo: Wilfrid Laurier University Press, 2006.

The Truth and Reconciliation Commission (TRC) of Canada. *Canada's Residential Schools: The History, Part 1, Origins to 1939, The Final Report of the Truth and Reconciliation Commission of Canada, Volume I.* Winnipeg: The Truth and Reconciliation Commission of Canada, 2015.

The Truth and Reconciliation Commission (TRC) of Canada. *Canada's Residential Schools: The History, Part 2, Origins to 1939, The Final Report of the Truth and Reconciliation Commission of Canada, Volume I.* Winnipeg: The Truth and Reconciliation Commission of Canada, 2015.

The Truth and Reconciliation Commission (TRC) of Canada. *Honouring the Truth, Reconciling for the Future Summary of the Final Report of the Truth and Reconciliation Commission of*

Canada. Winnipeg: The Truth and Reconciliation Commission of Canada, 2015.

Turnbull, Aleda. "Progressive Social Policy in Manitoba, 1915–1939." Master's Thesis, University of Manitoba, 1980.

Ursel, Jane. *Private Lives, Public Policy: 100 Years of State Intervention in the Family.* Toronto: Women's Press, 1992.

Chapter 8

Women Working Together:

The Native Women's Transition Centre

Annetta Armstrong and Josie Hill

> "The hardest time of my life was also the best time... I remember the Native Women's Transition Centre as being like a ray of sunshine in my life."—Lois Govereau-Kipling, former resident of NWTC

I (Josie Hill) was the executive director of the Native Women's Transition Centre (NWTC) from 1988 to 1992. I (Annetta Armstrong) am the current executive director of the centre, which is now known as the Indigenous Women's Healing Centre (IWHC). Incorporated in 1979, the NWTC officially opened its doors in 1981. In 1992 it moved from its original location on Selkirk Avenue to a new building on Aikins Street.

The organization has grown significantly from its early days on Selkirk Ave. The IWHC's North Star Lodge on Aikins Street is much larger than the original location and offers similar programs and services. The IWHC expanded with the development of Memengwaa Place, a second-stage housing facility located on Robinson Avenue. Memengwaa Place primarily provides housing for women that have completed the programming at North Star Lodge. The newest site, Eagle Women's Lodge, is located on Ellice Avenue. It provides housing for women in conflict with the law. In 2019, Eagle Women's Lodge became a Section 81 Healing Lodge for Indigenous women. This allows federally-sentenced women to serve their sentences in a secure and safe residential setting where they can access traditional programs and supports. Thousands of women have benefited from the services provided by the centre since 1981.

Although it is often described as an "emergency shelter" for Indigenous women, those who have worked at the centre have always thought of it as a home for women and their children, who have experienced far too much sadness in their young lives. Myrna Whitehawk, executive director of the centre from 1981 to 1982 describes the NWTC as a replacement for the traditional halfway house and a place for Indigenous women to find refuge.[1] Women come to the centre seeking safety from partner violence, but they have also been survivors of more insidious kinds of government-inflicted abuse. For example, many are survivors of the Sixties Scoop (see Chapter 7) and a child welfare system that remains systemically racist. Many are survivors of residential schools.

The stories we tell in this chapter build on interviews by Darrell Chippeway and Larry Morrissette conducted in 2013 as part of the Preserving the History of Aboriginal Institutional Development in Winnipeg project (see Chapter 1). In addition to those interviewed in 2013, we spoke with six women who were residents of the centre between 1981 and 2000, and two additional women who worked there.

The experiences of women who have turned to the NWTC for help and healing continue to be all too common. The National Inquiry into Missing and Murdered Indigenous Women and Girls (2019) describes the intergenerational and multigenerational trauma and social and economic marginalization endured by Indigenous women and girls. The report notes that "Indigenous girls, women and 2SLGBTQQIA

1 Penni Mitchell, "New Centre Offers a Helping Hand to Women," *Winnipeg Free Press*, October 26, 1981.

people are targeted by colonial violence embedded within institutions, structures, and systems, as well as interpersonal violence, where these encounters occur."[2] The inquiry report emphasizes the need for healing and describes its vision of healing to include "dignity, family participation, peer support and cultural safety." This philosophy has long been integrated into life at the NWTC.

The National Inquiry into Missing and Murdered Indigenous Women and Girls (MMIWG) gives evidence of the vulnerability and trauma experienced by Indigenous girls, women, and 2SLGBTQQIA that is as prevalent today as it was when the NWTC first opened its doors. In addition to the data and testimonials captured in the 2019 report of the National Inquiry into MMIWG, statistics show that Indigenous girls, women, and 2SLGBTQQIA remain extremely vulnerable to violence and systemic harm. The report found that sixty-three percent of Indigenous women have experienced physical or sexual assault in their lifetime, and ninety-one percent of children in foster care are Indigenous.[3] Until July 2020, the Manitoba government actively engaged in the practice of issuing "birth alerts." Birth alerts are used as a mechanism to notify hospitals and other child and family services (CFS) agencies of the need for further assessment before a newborn is discharged to the care of a parent who has been assessed as "high risk." Under this practice, a CFS agency issues the birth alert and Manitoba Families is responsible for the distribution of the alert.[4]

2 National Inquiry into Missing and Murdered Indigenous Women and Girls (Canada), *Reclaiming Power and Place: The Final Report of the National Inquiry into Missing and Murdered Indigenous Women and Girls*, Vol. 1a (Vancouver: Privy Council Office, 2019), 124. https://www.mmiwg-ffada.ca/final-report/.

3 Loanna Heindinger, *Violent Victimization and Perceptions of Safety: Experiences of First Nations, Métis and Inuit Women in Canada* (Statistics Canada Catalogue no. 85-002-x, 2022), https://www150.statcan.gc.ca/n1/en/pub/85-002-x/2022001/article/00004-eng.pdf?st=LffWs33.

4 Government of Manitoba, "End of Birth Alert Practice," accessed December 21, 2022, https://www.gov.mb.ca/fs/childfam/end-birth-alerts.html.

Despite the end of this practice, which has been highly criticized as discriminatory and unconstitutional, Indigenous children continue to be apprehended at a disproportionate rate, and the cycle of intergenerational trauma continues.

The Indian Métis Friendship Centre: Identifying a Need and Finding a Solution

As described in Chapter 2, the Indian and Métis Friendship Centre (IMFC) was the incubator of many Indigenous community initiatives in the latter part of the twentieth century. In the late 1970s, the IMFC identified the need for an emergency shelter for Indigenous women. Led at that time by director Mary Richard, the IMFC collaborated with other organizations to establish the Native Women's Transition Centre. I (Hill) recall learning about the NWTC's history from my mentor Mary Richard. In 1974, Richard moved from her position as the women's organizer of the IMFC to become its executive director.

Under Richard's leadership, in the mid-1970s, the IMFC along with the United Church hosted a conference to explore ways to support vulnerable young women aging out of the child welfare system. Disconnected from their communities and families, these young women were all too often preyed upon by older white men—trapped in violent and abusive relationships with nowhere to turn. I recall Mary Richard describing the conference—called "Women on the Skids"—that resulted in the initial commitment to establish residential services for Indigenous women. The Native Family Life Counselling Program Inc. established a committee to further develop the concept of a transition centre for Indigenous women. With support from the Indian and Métis Friendship Centre, the United Church of Canada and the Mennonite Central Committee, and with funding through Canada Employment, the NWTC was incorporated in 1979 and established at 367 Selkirk Avenue in 1981.

367 Selkirk Avenue—Where It All Began

A total of five women and their six children were the first residents to move into the centre in July 1981. The centre was funded by the federal Department of Employment and Immigration and Canadian Community Projects. The women were charged minimal room and board at the three-story house, which was owned by the United Church. They participated in household duties and had access to a number of programs, including "a native cultural program."[5] Designed as a temporary home for women in transition, the maximum length of stay—although somewhat flexible—was one year.

An important aspect of its programming was and is encouraging women to "return to their cultural roots." This mandate has expanded considerably since the centre was first established as a small safe home for Indigenous women and children. The initial location on Selkirk Avenue could accommodate twenty-one women and children for the maximum stay of one year. The women worked with staff to set goals and develop plans for independence. The centre offered a safe space to heal from the trauma resulting from violence and victimization, sexual abuse, and substance use. The centre offered support to women seeking to reclaim their children from the child welfare system. It offered opportunities to build capacity through community involvement, work opportunities through a catering social enterprise, and networking and relationship building within the Indigenous women's community.

According to Jackie Lavallee, the director of the NWTC from 1983 to 1988, the intention behind the centre was to make it feel as much as possible like home while also providing the women with guidance toward independent living.[6] She said the women residing at NWTC had faced lives full of challenges. Most had come through the child welfare system, and many had lost their children to that system. All of the women in the centre had endured a lifetime of poverty. They came to

5 Mitchell, "New Centre Offers a Helping Hand."

6 Davis, Anthony, "Centre Gives Women a New Start", *Winnipeg Free Press*, February 7, 1988.

the centre "simply stating that all they want for themselves, and their children is a better life than what they have known."[7] Lavallee concluded that the women's lives would start to turn around once they "begin to have hope and confidence to start making their own decisions and believe that they can provide a better life for themselves and their children."[8] Women residing at the centre were able to participate in a variety of programs and services, both within the home and in the community, including "drug and alcohol counselling, psychiatric therapy, family skills programs and financial education."[9]

Women we spoke with shared vivid memories of the old three-story house on Selkirk Avenue. People who lived and worked in the centre described it as a safe, warm, and welcoming place where they and their children found safety from abusive relationships—where they had access to counselling, programs, and where they learned new skills. They described the staff at the centre as kind, caring, and non-judgmental. Lois Govereau-Kipling recalls being able to talk freely without judgment:

> It was refreshing because you knew that they weren't going to go behind your back and call your [CFS] worker... that's the part that I liked. I could be myself and I could actually talk [about] how I felt and I wasn't being judged about it. So that gave me the freedom to be able to say how I felt and what I needed and, you know, not be scared.[10]

Vivian Ketchum lived at the centre in 1990. She recalls a "change" she felt when she first walked into the white building, which looked to her from the outside as more of a storefront business than a home. She remembers that "it didn't look like an institution at all... It didn't look too impressive, but there was a lot happening inside." Importantly, she too remembers being welcomed without judgment. She recalls the

7 Ibid.
8 Ibid.
9 Ibid.
10 Lois Govereau-Kipling interview by Josie Hill, May 2022.

"pure acceptance of who I was," and that "we were just really loved."[11] Sandy Alward lived at the centre in 1990. She was adopted by a non-Indigenous family when she was three years old and disconnected from her Indigenous roots. She says the NWTC was important because it connected her with other Indigenous people, and "it was the first place I was able to be myself, safely."[12]

Lainie Neal worked at the NWTC for about five years beginning in 1989. She was hired on contract to develop job descriptions for staff and later worked as the interim executive director and then stayed on as a board member. Like Ketchum, Neal recalls an old unimpressive building that was "brought to life" by the residents and staff. She recalls the staff room being next to the front door, and "anybody who walked in the front door got an enthusiastic welcome."

The main floor was a common space shared by staff and residents. It had a very large living room that was painted and decorated to resemble a rustic cabin. The living room was where we held ceremonies, watched TV, and had meetings. Also on the main floor was a large dining room where the women and children would share their meals. There was a small kitchen and bathroom, and a large pantry off the dining room.

As is often the case, the kitchen was the heart of the home. Ketchum recalls having sleepless nights and going down to the kitchen where she sat with staff. She said, "I would go [into the office near the kitchen] and just sit there. They wouldn't say nothing. They just let me sit there... they were really, really, supportive." She talks about going down there late at night and early in the morning so "the other girls wouldn't see me cry." But Ketchum also found the kitchen "scary as heck" because she "didn't know what to do in there."[13]

The basement was laid out over two levels. A playroom filled with toys and activities for the kids was situated on the first level. Further down was a dark second level where the administrative office was

11 Ibid.

12 Sandy Alward interview by Josie Hill, May 2022.

13 Vivian Ketchum interview by Josie Hill, May 2022.

located. Ketchum describes the offices in the basement as "small and comforting." Neal also remembers the office and the low ceilings, which "could be dangerous if you were tall." She laughed when recalling the time when "a messenger who was a little too tall banged his head coming down the stairs on the ceiling. So I had to do first aid and slap a Band-Aid on his forehead!"[14]

The second floor had four bedrooms and a large bathroom with a very large clawfoot tub. The large bathtub was an important feature—everyone seemed to have something to say about it. We were able to bathe a few kids at a time in that tub and even used it as a make-shift little swimming pool for the kids to cool off in when temperatures soared in the summer months. But Lavallee reminded us that the bathtub wasn't ideal: "If you were bathing your baby, it was hard ... so a lot of them would use the [bathroom] off the kitchen for bathing babies."[15]

The third floor was one large single room where women with larger families would stay. Govereau-Kipling recalls living on the third floor with her children.

Life at the centre was busy. The women mostly got along well. There was a lot of joking and teasing. Staff and families celebrated birthdays and special occasions. Staff kept busy getting women to various appointments, including counselling and meetings with various workers. Everyone was up early in the morning getting kids off to school. The women would participate in various support programs at the centre. Staff made time to take the women and children on day trips to the beach and other fun places. Most of the women who came to the centre had children, and much of the activities centered on them. They brought the centre to life—ensured it felt like home. Neal describes a day in the life at the centre as "fun ... we worked hard and we played hard. And there was also lots of laughing. It was a homey place where people felt welcomed and cared for. And I saw healing happening there."[16]

14 Lainie Neal interview by Josie Hill, May 2022.

15 Jackie Lavallee interview by Josie Hill, May 2022

16 Ibid.

Catering and Learning to Cook With Isobel Monkman

Over lunch with Jackie Lavallee, we talked about the many programs and services offered at the centre over the years. We asked Lavallee about her memories of the catering business and how it began. She recalled:

> NWTC made bannock so well...we used to get contacted by the Native Caucus [Indigenous MLAs] of the provincial government. They had their own caucus meetings and I guess they'd have them regularly, but they would contact us and say, "can your group make bannock for such and such a date...we need some butter and some jam"... And we did that all the time.

After providing the caucus with bannock on several occasions, Lavallee was approached by a representative to cater a banquet at the Friendship Centre.

> The Native Caucus in government, they were doing a fundraising thing for Howard Pawley. He was Premier then...And so they contacted us to do the food prep for this big banquet...[but we didn't] have the resources to do that. We were making this good bannock for them, so they knew we had something going, right? Elaine Cowan...was a special assistant to Elijah Harper [NDP MLA and Cabinet Minister]. She came to see me.
>
> I said, you know we can't do this banquet. We do not have any transportation, equipment...She pulls this wad of money out of her purse. She said, here. I've got $4,000 here. This is what you can use to start up buying your supplies...I said, "I don't know...I need to talk to the group like I can't just go ahead and commit us to something"...I approached the staff and some of the residents and they're going—well maybe we can.
>
> So, [it took] some organizing, right? We went to the Friendship Centre and used their big kitchen...It was hard work. We did such a damn good job and so much so that while we were packing up and

> cleaning dishes and stuff, we were all called out to and got a standing ovation and flowers from the organizers. And so that felt really good.
>
> So we were able to pay off all our [bills] and were able to pay everybody who worked for every minute that they worked. We were able to pay the women that babysat. And then we're going, Oh my God, there is money left! What are we going to do with it? This is just incredible.
>
> We had quite a bit of money. So we as a group said, okay, let's put half of it into getting supplies to the center like craft activities, all kinds of stuff. And even we keep half of it to sort of build some capital, maybe we got a business thing going on and we need to buy some of that stuff.
>
> And that's how the catering started. After that everybody would call us.
>
> Not only did it compensate the centre and the workers, but it gave something else to the women. We saw that we could do this, and their pride in completing a job and then the learning process.[17]

Isobel Monkman stands out in our memories of NWTC. Monkman was hired by the NWTC as a cook in 1988. She worked at the Selkirk Avenue house and later at the Aikins location. While working, she moved into the second-stage Memengwaa Place where she was the house mom. When I (Hill) was the executive director at Ma Mawi Wi Chi Itata Centre, I convinced Monkman to join us as a house mom at our adolescent mothers' home. She passed away while working there and we later named the home after her. It is now known as Isobel's Place.

Isobel Monkman was a talented cook who loved to share her skills with the NWTC residents. She was smart and loving, with a quick wit. Her cooking prowess led to the establishment of what we believe to have been the first Indigenous women-led social enterprise in Winnipeg. The business was incorporated and increasingly recognized by the community. Most of the catering was for other community organizations hosting meetings, workshops, and conferences.

17 Ibid.

NWTC residents and staff provided the catering for the release of the Aboriginal Justice Inquiry report. This was significant given the women's entanglement in the oppressive systems described in the report (see Chapter 7).

The catering business became an important source of income for the centre as well as for the residents who worked in the catering business. Most of the residents received minimal income through the city of Winnipeg's social assistance program. Through the catering business, we were able to give them a bit of money so that they could buy some things for themselves and their children that they otherwise could not afford. But it wasn't just about money. The women gained self-confidence serving at events, meeting new people, and being recognized by their customers for the great food and service they offered. Their involvement in the catering business opened a new world to them. It was meaningful to them to feel a sense of belonging to the community and to be recognized for their work.

Monkman fully engaged the residents in the operations of the catering business. In addition to the small amount of money provided directly to the women, the business enabled the centre to support several extra initiatives for the women. We purchased a van, hired summer staff, and sent the women and kids on the Pow Wow Trail. We rented cabins and took individual families out to enjoy some quiet family time on their own. We were able to take the staff and women to a conference in B.C. for a week, and we were able to use the proceeds from the business for Christmas and birthday celebrations. In addition to the financial benefits, the catering business proved to be therapeutic. Many hours were spent sitting around the table peeling potatoes, chopping vegetables, and making bannock, all the while sharing stories and laughing as the women worked together preparing food.

Whether it was the catering business or cooking meals with the residents, everyone remembers Monkman and the kitchen. Rosaleen Flett said she didn't know anything about cooking before she moved to the NWTC. She recalls that everyone had to participate in meal preparation "and I'm not a very good cook, especially for a big crowd. I was always screwing up the meals around supper time! I was always trying to pawn it off to somebody else," she said laughing. "Isobel helped me. I learned to make my sweet and sour ribs from her. She showed me how she did it." Flett laughed when describing Isobel's instructions: "Just throw it in, throw it in. Eyeball it!"[18]

Lainie Neal also fondly recalls Monkman and the catering business:

> Oh yeah. I got chubby...they made extra money doing catering for other organizations in the community. And we had the best cook on the planet. And she always whipped up bannock and stew and rice pudding and you name it, it was delicious. And we all got fat! And made some money for the organization. So, yeah, that was Isobel's baby, and she was the best at it. She was such an integral part of what happened there from day to day. And the women adored her.[19]

Debbie Govereau lived at the centre from 1991 to 1992. She also recalls participating in the catering business. She agreed that it was hard work but said, "who cares! We had a little bit of extra money, and it boosted up our self-confidence."[20]

The Move to Aikins Street

When I (Hill) became the NWTC's executive director in 1988, it was apparent that the centre needed a new building. Due to the volume of activity and the number of residents over the years, the house was getting run down, was bursting at the seams, and it didn't feel safe. We worried that if there were a fire, not all of the women and children would be able to escape. I recall waking up in cold sweats having nightmares about fire in the building. It would also get unbearably hot, especially on the third floor. I recall a mom with her five young children living on the third floor in that unbearable heat. The fire alarm

18 Rosaleen Flett interview by Josie Hill, May 2022.
19 Lainie Neal interview by Josie Hill, May 2022.
20 Debbie Govereau interview by Josie Hill, May 2022.

kept going off on the third floor because it was so hot and humid. So I pulled out the Yellow Pages and started to phone air conditioning places. I spoke with one guy and said—you know my name is this, and this is where I work and this is what's happening and we don't have any money but we'd sure like air conditioning and we'll get the money and pay for it but we don't have it now—and the guy said, "you know what ... I'll come and do it." So, they came and put air conditioning in and that was really nice.

But that was a band-aid solution. We believed the women and their children deserved better, and I worked with the board of directors to explore other options. In 1988, the United Church, which owned the building, decided to sell. We contemplated buying it, but we thought that the asking price of $63,000 was too high. The cost of repairing it up to safety standards was upwards of $150,000. I recall we invested quite a bit to maintain the deteriorating house—it seemed like there was always something needing fixing. At a board/staff retreat, Glenn Cochrane, who was the chair of the board, suggested we build our own home. So that is what we decided to do.

And so the next phase of the NWTC began. The women were fully involved in the process from attending meetings with funders to choosing paint colours and furnishings. We had many battles with government departments, who seemed determined to make it near impossible for us to achieve our goals. We eventually raised the money we needed and began the process of building. We were adamant that the project would be a fully Indigenous project. We hired Métis Housing Inc. as the contractor, and they were very good to us. At the end of the project, they gave us $10,000 to help with other costs, and they added a few extras to the building. When we opened the doors of our new centre, we were one of the first Indigenous organizations to own our own building. We were so proud to be able to offer women and children the home that they deserved.

Soon after the building was completed in 1992, I felt it was time for me to move on. Lucille Bruce succeeded me as the executive director of the NWTC, and under her leadership, a second-stage housing facility was built on land purchased earlier, adjacent to the centre. Bruce was the executive director at NWTC on and off for close to twenty years. In an interview with Darrell Chippeway and Larry Morrissette in 2012, she describes her time at the centre: "I absolutely thrived on it, and I loved it because I had an opportunity to do things that I would not have had an opportunity to do elsewhere, and that was to be a part of creating a continuum of services in the North End community."[21] With the new building completed, the women living at the centre expressed an interest in additional programs in the neighbourhood, emphasizing the needs of children and youth. The NWTC, along with the North End Women's Centre and Ikwe Widdjiitiwin (Indigenous women's crisis shelter), agreed to establish, as Bruce describes, "a continuum of supports and services for families in our community."

Prior to my (Hill) departure, we set our sights on building a safe place for youth. Ndinawemaaganag Endaawaad (Ndinawe) Inc. was established in 1993 as a project of NWTC, and later became a not-for-profit organization dedicated to helping at-risk youth in Winnipeg. As it explains on its website homepage, it continues to provide a range of services, "connecting vulnerable children and youth aged 11–17 with the shelter, culture, recreation, education, outreach and support they need for safe and healthy lives." After Ndinawe was established, Bruce collaborated with sister organizations to fill other gaps in service. The women-led organizations created White Butterfly (Wabshke Memengwaa) Place, a residential facility for girls, which would later become part of a network of supports for youth under Project Neecheewam: Resources for Family and Youth.

In 1989, NWTC, North End Women's Centre (NEWC), and Ikwe Widdjiitiwin established Wahbung Abinoonjiiag, an organization

21 Lucille Bruce interview by Darrell Chippeway and Larry Morrissette, 8 December 2012.

focused on supporting Indigenous children who had witnessed family violence. In 2003, this group also established Oyate Tipi Cumini Yape, which provided donated household goods and furniture to women and their children leaving residential organizations.

Transitions: Learning, Healing, and Moving Forward

Betty Maud, whose Spirit name is Helping Eagle Woman, was a resident at the centre in 1985 and again in 1992. She describes having gone through many transitions in her life as a residential school survivor, "but the Native Woman's Transition Centre was the one that started it all for me and all my journey."[22]

It's impossible to know where all the women's journeys took them after they moved on. Some, like Lois Govereau-Kipling and Betty Maud, have gone on to work in the community with children and women. Vivian Ketchum is actively engaged in community advocacy work. In a 2000 profile of the NWTC, one resident at Memengwaa Place, the centre's second-stage housing program, speaks of her experience: "I started attending the programs at Native Women's Transition Centre, and the walls I had built around myself slowly started to come down. For the first time, I began to learn about the cycle of violence and how I was involved in it. It was then I made the decision to stop it from continuing on to my children." She describes her transition to a "sober and drug-free lifestyle" and how she provided a safe home for her children: "my children know they are safe in their home and that I can finally provide stability for them."[23] Another resident describes the pain of having lost her children to the child welfare system. She had lost hope of getting them back until she met a worker at the NWTC. Soon after, she became a resident at the centre and gained the strength to fight to have her children returned. With help from the centre staff and various programs, she describes becoming a stronger person. At

22 Betty Maud interview by Josie Hill, May 2022.

23 Vivian Ketchum interview by Josie Hill, May 2022.

the time of her interview, she looked forward to having her children returned to her "this summer."

Another describes her journey with NWTC and the support she received to reclaim her children from the child welfare system. She adds that her involvement with the NWTC gave her an opportunity to "get involved with community issues ... With the help of Native Women's Transition Centre and the continued support at Memengwaa Place, I believe I have truly found myself."[24] Another resident describes feeling like a "failure" when losing her children to the child welfare system in 1996. After leaving a twelve-year abusive relationship, she embarked on a long journey to overcome deeply rooted traumas with the help of many community organizations, but, she explains,

> It was through the Native Women's Transition centre that I continued my journey. I learned more about where my anger came from, through sharing circles which focused on topics such as family of origin, colonization, the cycle of violence and intergenerational issues. This helped me not only in a healing process but also in learning how to forgive myself.[25]

In our recent conversation with Govereau-Kipling, she said, "To be honest, I don't know if I would have my kids now if I wasn't in the Centre ... You had people helping you, navigating, and sticking up for you ... That's the part that really helped me go through life." Ketchum said, "I think the Transition Centre saved my life." When asked if she had a message for other Indigenous women struggling with addiction and violence in their lives, she said, "... it will save your life and your children."[26]

Rosaleen Flett was a resident at the Selkirk Avenue home and later stayed in second-stage housing. When asked if she had a message for other Indigenous women needing support, she said:

24 Ibid, 49.

25 Ibid, 50.

26 Vivian Ketchum interview by Josie Hill May 2022.

> I'd like to say... when you're scared of somebody and feeling you need somebody, it's always a place to go to. There is open arms, understanding people who will listen, and they've got lots of programs that will help in all different ways. Spiritually, physically... and all kinds of programs to help identify yourself as an Indigenous woman.[27]

Since opening its doors, the NWTC, now the IWHC, has offered a safe place for thousands of Indigenous women and their children. Regardless of where their lives took them, we believe that their time at NWTC made an important difference in their lives. A new generation of Indigenous women at the IWHC continue the work of the NWTC, having been mentored by those that came before them. And they are now mentoring the next generation of Indigenous women who will lead this important organization into the future.

Indigenous women-led centres like the Native Women's Transition Centre continue to be important sources of support and healing. At the Indigenous Women's Healing Centre, a new generation of women now carries on the work of the women who came before them. Honouring the history of the women who paved the way is an important part of our journey.

Bibliography

Alward, Sandy. Interview by Josie Hill. May 2022.

Bruce, Lucille. Interview by Darrell Chippeway and Larry Morrissette, 8 December 2012. Recording at University of Manitoba Archives and Special Collections. Winnipeg, MB.

Chartrand, Cheyenne. Native Women's Transition Centre, 2000. https://chodarr.org/sites/default/files/chodarr0027.pdf.

Davis, Anthony. "Centre Gives Women a New Start", *Winnipeg Free Press*, February 7, 1988.

Flett, Rosaleen. Interview by Josie Hill, May 2022.

27 Rosaleen Flett interview by Josie Hill May 2022.

Govereau, Debbie. Interview by Josie Hill, May 2022.
Govereau-Kipling, Lois. Interview by Josie Hill, May 2022.
Government of Manitoba. "End of Birth Alert Practice." Accessed December 21, 2022.
https://www.gov.mb.ca/fs/childfam/end-birth-alerts.html.
Heindinger, Loanna. *Violent Victimization and Perceptions of Safety: Experiences of First Nations, Métis and Inuit Women in Canada.* Juristat Article. Statistics Canada Catalogue no. 85-002-x, 2022. https://www150.statcan.gc.ca/n1/en/pub/85-002-x/2022001/article/00004-eng.pdf?st=LffWs33.
Ketchum, Vivian. Interview by Josie Hill. May 2022.
Lavallee, Jackie. Interview by Josie Hill. May 2022.
Maud, Betty. Interview by Josie Hill. May 2022.
Mitchell, Penni. "New Centre Offers a Helping Hand to Women." *Winnipeg Free Press,* October 26, 1981.
Neal, Lainie. Interview by Josie Hill. May 2022.
National Inquiry into Missing and Murdered Indigenous Women and Girls (Canada). *Reclaiming Power and Place: The Final Report of the National Inquiry into Missing and Murdered Indigenous Women and Girls.* Volume 1a. Vancouver: Privy Council Office, 2019. https://www.mmiwg-ffada.ca/final-report/.

Chapter 9

Two-Spirit Resistance and Resurgence in Winnipeg

Chantal Fiola and Albert McLeod

In her 2018 book *Prairie Fairies: A History of Queer Communities and People in Western Canada, 1930–1985*, Valerie Korinek identifies a timeline of queer activism in major Canadian cities up to 1985 when the AIDS epidemic reached Canada. She notes that in Winnipeg starting in the 1930s, various urban spaces (riverbanks, public toilets, hotel bars) became inscribed as queer spaces. After World War II, gay male networks were formed, and house parties and lounges enabled lesbian women to participate in queer subculture as well. By the late 1960s, gay bars, organizations, and activism began in earnest with the latter becoming integrated into the larger queer movement in Canada via conferences, periodicals, and organizations. Korinek's contribution to queer history on the prairies is invaluable; however, queer Indigenous voices are nearly absent in her narrative.

This gap in the literature regarding Indigenous contributions to queer activism in Winnipeg, Manitoba (and beyond) is also apparent in Aaron Floresco's 2014 documentary *One Gay City: A History of*

LGBT Life in Winnipeg, which ignores Two-Spirit (2S) people.[1] Years later, after receiving criticism, Floresco added two queer Indigenous interviews to the end of the documentary. Similarly, Korinek acknowledges that "of all the fragments of histories woven together in this book, the absence of Indigenous gays and lesbians haunts me most."[2]

Our chapter highlights Indigenous 2SLGBTQ resistance and resurgence in Winnipeg. We offer a concise Indigenous-centered history of the 2SLGBTQ movement in Winnipeg reaching back to pre-colonial times but focusing on the 1970s to the present. Eight longstanding Indigenous 2SLGBTQ advocates living in Winnipeg, including 2S elders and one 2S youth, were interviewed for this chapter. They discuss becoming involved in the 2S movement, their 2S activism over the years, their greatest challenges, the role of Indigenous spirituality in 2S resurgence, and what they see on the horizon for 2SLGTBQ people. Experiencing more than their share of heartache due to colonialism, homo/transphobia, and lateral violence, they also speak of hard-earned triumphs, joys, and self-acceptance. Their stories paint a picture of the evolution of 2S resistance and resurgence in Winnipeg over the past fifty years, including the development and maintenance of longstanding 2S organizations.

1 Aaron Floresco, dir., *One Gay City: A History of LGBT Life in Winnipeg* (Winnipeg: Past Perfect Productions, 2014), DVD. Note: *Two-Spirit (2S)* recalls Indigenous nation–specific conceptions of genders, sexualities, and people who identify on the lesbian, gay, bisexual, transgender, queer (LGBTQ), non-binary, and gender nonconforming spectrum.

2 One exception is Korinek's discussion of Annie Maude "Nan" McKay, a Métis lesbian (who did not publicly identify as either) born in 1892 in the Northwest Territories. The first Indigenous woman to graduate from the University of Saskatchewan, she was profiled by the university in 2007; she is featured kissing her friend Hope Weir on the cover of Korinek's book. Valerie Korinek, *Prairie Fairies: A History of Queer Communities and People in Western Canada, 1930–1985* (Toronto: University of Toronto Press, 2018), 341. Also see Valerie Korinek, "'We're the Girls of the Pansy Parade': Historicizing Winnipeg's Queer Subcultures, 1930s–1970," *Social History* 45, 89 (2012): 117–155.

But first, allow us to introduce ourselves: we are Albert McLeod (she/he) and Chantal Fiola (she/her). Albert, an internationally recognized 2S Cree elder, has dedicated thirty-five years to 2SLGBTQ activism in Winnipeg and abroad. A pioneer in the 2S movement, she helped found the Two-Spirited People of Manitoba (TSPM), dedicated many years to HIV/AIDS advocacy, and remains active with the International Council of Two-Spirit Societies (ICTSS).[3] In 2018, he received an Honorary Doctor of Laws from the University of Winnipeg in recognition of her lifetime of advocacy. Chantal is 2S Michif (Red River Métis) with family from the historic Métis community of St. Laurent, Manitoba. She is an Associate Professor at the University of Winnipeg whose research centers Métis identity, spirituality, and methodology, and Indigenous genders and sexualities. In 2018, she was crowned the International Two-Spirit Ogichidaakwe (Warrior Woman) at the 31st International Two-Spirit Gathering, and in 2019, she became the interim chair and founding secretary-treasurer of the Two-Spirit Michif Local of the Manitoba Métis Federation.

A Brief History of the 2SLGBTQ Movement in Winnipeg

Gender and sexual diversity were common in Indigenous nations precontact.[4] During early contact, Indigenous 2SLGBTQ people

3 In 2022, this organization changed its name to 2Spirit Manitoba; at the time of writing, this is not yet common knowledge; therefore, we continue using *Two-Spirited People of Manitoba* in this chapter—except in one instance discussing the organization's activities post-name change.

4 Chantal Fiola, "Naawenangweyaabeg Coming In: Intersections of Indigenous Sexuality and Spirituality," in *In Good Relation: History, Gender, and Kinship in Indigenous Feminisms*, ed. Sarah Nickel and Amanda Fehr, 136–153 (Winnipeg: University of Manitoba Press, 2020); Duane Brayboy, "Two-Spirits, One Heart, Five Genders," *Indian Country Today Media Network*, January 23, 2016, http://indiancountrytodaymedianetwork.com/2016/01/23/two-spirits-one-heart-five-genders; Alex Wilson, "N'tacimowin inna nah': Our Coming in Stories," *Canadian Woman Studies* 26, no. 3–4 (2008): 193–199, http://cws.journals.yorku.ca/index.php/cws/article/viewFile/22131/20785; Sue-Ellen Jacobs, Wesley Thomas, and Sabine Lang, *Two-Spirit People: Native American Gender Identity, Sexuality, and Spirituality* (Chicago: University of Illinois Press, 1997).

would have likely been present in the fur trade and relations within the Red River Settlement despite their erasure in colonial texts. In the 1888 poem "Last of the Bison," Charles Mair (antagonist to Louis Riel and Métis sovereignty) identifies a "burdash" (sic) bison as the protagonist in his narrative lamenting the demise of the great bison herds.[5] While Mair references a colonial term, one wonders if Métis and First Nation bison hunters tried teaching him their concept of a gender-diverse being. 2S Métis Anishinaabe scholar, Dr Kai Pyle, has scoured the archives and uncovered 2S Métis, Anishinaabe, Cree, and Dene ancestors from the 1790s to the 1950s who lived outside colonially-defined cishetero norms of gender and sexuality, including: Ozaawindib, Antoine Clement, Elise Taupier Houle, piyesiwiskwew, Mary Duchesne, Annie Maude McKay, and Beulah Brunelle.[6]

The late Anishinaabemowin (Ojibwe language) specialist Roger Roulette informed us that Anishinaabe worldview accepts human creation as intentionally constructed by Spirit (of the natural world) and inclusive of diverse genders and sexualities. According to Roulette, the term *aawi* means "he/she is who he/she is supposed to be,"[7] and *agookwe* means "a hidden woman" or a female identity-spirit within a biologically male body. Indigenous languages confirm 2SLGBTQ people's existence since early human history.[8]

Colonization attempted to eradicate Indigenous genders and sexualities which did not conform to EuroChristian binaries (male/female, homo/heterosexual). Anti-sodomy laws introduced by Henry VIII and affirmed by his daughter Queen Elizabeth I were exported by the

5 Quoted in "Charles Mair," in *Canadian Poets*, ed. John W. Garvin (Toronto: McClelland, Goodchild and Steward, 1916), 21-22.

6 Kai Pyle. "We Were There Too! Queer, Trans, and 2Spirit Métis History," 5 May 2022. Mawachihitotaak Métis Studies Symposium, 3-6 May 2022. Hybrid Zoom & Winnipeg, MB.

7 Anishinaabemowin and Nêhiyawewin (Cree) have animate and inanimate designations (rather than gender); the inanimate form is *aawiwan*, or "it is what it's supposed to be." Roger Roulette, personal communication, 2017.

8 Fiola, "Naawenangweyaabeg Coming In," 140.

British to their North American colonies.[9] Indian agents and priests then imposed heteronormative patriarchy onto Indigenous peoples. 2SLGBTQ roles and identities were further erased through institutions such as Indian Residential and Day Schools for more than a century. The outlawing of off-reserve mobility, ceremonies, and midwifery forced many Indigenous people to convert to Christianity and internalize homo/transphobia. Until the 1960s, Two-Spirit people were hidden within their communities—sometimes tolerated, sometimes oppressed, and occasionally protected.

In 1969, queer advocacy resulted in the Stonewall riots in New York and Prime Minister Pierre Trudeau amending the Criminal Code of Canada, decriminalizing homosexual acts between consenting adults in private.[10] In 1987, Manitoba became the first prairie province to prohibit discrimination based on sexual orientation via Bill 47 of their provincial human rights code.[11] Yet, mainstream queer culture privileged white cisgender gay males and erased Black and Indigenous People of Colour (BIPOC) contributions.

Since the 1960s, 2SLGBTQ people have been migrating from rural communities to Winnipeg, hoping to find a better life in the urban gay community. By the mid-1980s, a core group of people established a small, supportive Indigenous queer community. In 1986, the Nichiwakan Native Gay Society[12] was founded by Albert McLeod, Roger Armitte, and Myra Laramee after two young gay men in their circle died by suicide. In 2003, this society would be incorporated as the Two-Spirited People of Manitoba by Albert McLeod, Donna Glover, and Wilfred Abigosis, with a mission to improve the quality of life of

9 William Eskridge, *Dishonorable Passions: Sodomy Laws in America, 1861–2003* (Toronto: Penguin Group, 2008).

10 Stuart Chambers, "Pierre Elliott Trudeau and Bill C-150: A Rational Approach to Homosexual Acts, 1968–69," *Journal of Homosexuality* 57, 2 (2010): 249.

11 Korinek, *Prairie Fairies*, 296.

12 *Nichiwakan* means "my friend" in Cree.

Two-Spirit people in Manitoba through fundraising, advocacy, education, health services, housing, employment training, and cultural development. Collaborating with Winnipeg's Gays for Equality and Giovanni's Room (a gay cabaret), they began hosting alcohol-free "Tea and Bannock Socials." In 1987, the society participated in Winnipeg's first gay pride march, then in the inaugural International Two-Spirit Gathering in Minneapolis in 1988. In 1990, the society organized the third annual International Two-Spirit Gathering in Beausejour, Manitoba. There, Myra Laramee (a 2S elder featured in this chapter) shared a vision she received, which resulted in widespread adoption of the term *Two-Spirit.* [13] In 2018, at the thirty-first Annual International Two-Spirit Gathering in Manitoba, board of directors' elections were held for the 2Spirits in Motion Society (2SinMotion), the only national 2SLGBTQ organization in Canada. [14]

In November 2017, Prime Minister Justin Trudeau apologized to 2SLGBTQ Canadians for state-sponsored homophobic discrimination; [15] in the lead up to this, he established the "LGBTQ2 Secretariat." Other efforts to better relationships with 2S people in Canada included the Truth and Reconciliation Commission's (TRC) Winnipeg and Toronto forums for 2S residential school survivors, but 2S people were excluded from the TRC's 94 Calls to Action. The National Inquiry into Missing and Murdered Indigenous Women and Girls initially excluded queer people; however, 2S needs are incorporated throughout the 231 Calls for Justice (MMIW 2019). [16]

13 Fiola, "Naawenangweyaabeg Coming In," 139-140.

14 Upon incorporation in 2020, their name changed from 2Spirits in Motion Foundation to 2Spirits in Motion Society.

15 Read the apology here: Justin Trudeau, "Remarks by Prime Minster Justin Trudeau to Apologize to LGBTQ2 Canadians," Prime Minster of Canada Justin Trudeau website, November 28, 2017, https://pm.gc.ca/en/news/speeches/2017/11/28/remarks-prime-minister-justin-trudeau-apologize-lgbtq2-canadians.

16 In June 2018, Albert, on behalf of the TSPM, gave testimony to the Inquiry as an expert witness.

Indigenous governments have also attempted to support 2SLGBTQ people. At the 2018 Assembly of First Nations (AFN) General Assembly in Vancouver, delegate Chief Allan Polchies Jr. of St. Mary's First Nation and 2S elder Ed Lavallee initiated a resolution for the AFN to support the development and subsequent funding of the 2Spirits in Motion Society—it passed unanimously.[17] In August 2019, the Manitoba Métis Federation (MMF) announced the Two-Spirit Michif Local (2SML), which represents Métis 2SLGBTQ people primarily in Winnipeg—the first of its kind in a Métis governance structure in Canada. In December 2020, thanks to 2SML's advocacy, the MMF unanimously passed a resolution allowing Manitoba Métis citizens to identify as non-binary/gender nonconforming on their citizenship card.

Likewise, universities are trying to be responsive to 2SLGBTQ people. For example, the University of Winnipeg maintains a Two-Spirit Archives Collection and, in 2017, hosted a national conference titled Two-Spirit & Queer People of Colour: A Call to Conversation with LGBTQ & Allies, which produced its own Calls to Action.[18] We applaud these efforts, though much work is still needed.

Introducing the 2S Advocates

The eight individuals interviewed for this study are long-time 2SLGBTQ[19] advocates who have been involved in the 2S movement

17 Chief Allan Polchies Jr. was the first openly gay chief.

18 View the 2S Archives here: "Two-Spirit Archives," The University of Winnipeg, accessed December 26, 2022, https://archives.uwinnipeg.ca/our-collections/two-spirit-archives.html. Chantal Fiola co-chaired the conference. View the Calls to Action here: *The Findings of C2C: Two Spirit & Queer/Trans People of Colour; Calls to Action 2019* (conference findings from C2C: Two-Spirit & Queer/Trans People of Colour, the University of Winnipeg, Winnipeg, MB, October 20–22, 2017, Chantal Fiola and Sharanpal Ruprai, co-chairs, 2019), https://www.uwinnipeg.ca/c2c/docs/c2c_calls-to-action_final.pdf.

19 We refer to them as *Two-Spirit* for readability. They have chosen to use their real names.

since the 1970s.[20] Each accepted our *asemaa* (tobacco) and generously share their experiences below.

Albert McLeod is Cree with ancestry from Nisichawayasihk Cree Nation (Nelson House) and grew up in the Métis community of Cormorant and in The Pas, in northern Manitoba. He identifies as a cisgender, gay male with "a feminine or a female-oriented social engagement [style]. [I am] both male and female [and] I use the term Two-Spirit as my core identity" and she/he pronouns.

Dr. Myra Laramee, a "Métis, Cree, Ojibwe woman" with Scottish heritage, grew up in Winnipeg's North End. Despite bringing the term *Two-Spirit* to the queer Indigenous community, Laramee avoids labels. Adhering to her father's advice to her upon coming out, she does not discount men or women as life partners.

Barbara Bruce, like Laramee and McLeod, is recognized as a 2S elder; she was awarded the Order of Manitoba in 2018. She is a citizen of the Métis Nation and grew up in the historic Métis community of St. Laurent, Manitoba. She identifies as a Two-Spirit woman and has been instrumental in the development of a 2S Métis community in Winnipeg.

Gayle Pruden, a 2S elder, is Ojibwe from Little Saskatchewan First Nation with treaty rights through Pinaymootang (Fairford) First Nation. Pruden explains, "I live as female 24/7 but I [was born] male. I never had anything done, as in changing what I was born with, but I'm comfortable living as a female." She does not mind the terms *trans* and *Two-Spirit* but generally avoids labels.

Jamie Goulet is becoming recognized as a 2S elder. She is a citizen of the Métis Nation and grew up in a Métis settlement near Kississing Lake and The Pas in northern Manitoba. Goulet identifies as "an old dyke!"—she also used to use the term *lesbian*.

Lorne Olson is Ojibwe from Brokenhead First Nation. He identifies as a [cisgender] gay male. He explains, "I just identify as gay. But

20 All except Sadie-Phoenix, the 2S youth.

formally, since the Two-Spirit term came about, I found that that term fit the most. It fit all of me."

Connie Merasty is Swampy Cree from Opaskwayak Cree Nation and was born and raised near The Pas, Manitoba. Responding to the question of how she identifies in terms of gender and sexuality, Merasty says, "I am Two-Spirited. My identity is Two-Spirit, and I identify as a transgender woman."

The youngest person to speak with us was Sadie-Phoenix Lavoie, who is Anishinaabe from Sagkeeng First Nation. Lavoie identifies as genderfluid and bisexual and uses they/them pronouns.

Despite limitations in time and funding, we are pleased with the diversity of voices represented in this chapter, including Anishinaabe, Cree, and Métis—Indigenous nations whose territory became southern Manitoba and Winnipeg. They helped establish and maintain longstanding 2SLGBTQ organizations and illuminate 2S activism in Winnipeg.

Becoming Involved in the 2S Movement

The 2S advocates herein identify several avenues through which they first became involved in the 2S movement: they discuss their advocacy surrounding the HIV/AIDS epidemic in the 1980s and the importance of creating safer spaces for 2SLGBTQ; and they discuss their involvement in nascent 2SLGBTQ organizations, in the Indigenous women's movement, and in the transgender movement.

In Winnipeg, the Nichiwakan Native Gay Society was involved in the development of the Village Clinic, specializing in HIV/AIDS. Glen Murray, an educator from Village Clinic (who later became Winnipeg's first openly gay mayor), recruited Laramee and McLeod to provide HIV/AIDS education to First Nation communities across Manitoba. In 1993, a group of 2S volunteers established the non-profit organization Manitoba Aboriginal AIDS Task Force (MAATF), which amalgamated into the Nine Circles Community Health Centre in 2001. Laramee and McLeod were also members of the first provincial AIDS advisory committee. In 1997, the Canadian Aboriginal AIDS Network (CAAN) was created—Pruden and Merasty remain active therein.

In our interviews with Connie Merasty and Lorne Olson, each spoke of the devastating impacts of the HIV/AIDS epidemic upon the queer community in Winnipeg and identified underlying issues such as poverty, homelessness, addictions, crime, sex trade work, and child sexual exploitation. Many personally know 2SLGBTQ people who died from HIV/AIDS, suicide, drug overdose, or murder. Recalling his experience with homelessness after moving to Winnipeg, Olson shares,

> It was more or less survival all the time: How can I survive another month? Then I'd find another group to hang out with for a while... I was really lucky. I didn't get completely consumed by that street life, drugs, crime. But, in general, most of those kids were Two-Spirited that I ended up with.

Stories of 2S youth moving to the city and struggling with these issues are portrayed in the 1998 production *Hectic,* written by Margaret Sweatman in collaboration with current and former sex workers from Winnipeg, and in Noam Gonick's 2004 film *Stryker,* based in Winnipeg's North End. Merasty was one of the trans actresses featured in both. Everyone we spoke with first became involved in the 2S movement out of necessity and survival.

From the 1970s to the early 2000s, Winnipeg social clubs and bars were among the only safe spaces for 2SLGBTQ. Early Winnipeg gay bars such as Giovanni's Room (Gio's; 1982–2013), Happenings Social Club (1970–2009), The Detour (1978–1980), and the lesbian bar Ms. Purdy's (1983–2002), were spaces where one could first meet other 2SLGBTQ people and form community. The 2S advocates we spoke with participated in these clubs and contributed to their longevity—these clubs outlasted most other queer institutions across Canada.[21] Gender fluidity

21 Korinek, *Prairie Fairies,* 156-157. Noticeably absent from their stories was the Campus Gay Club, later named Gays for Equality, then Winnipeg Gay and Lesbian Resource Centre, and finally, Rainbow Resource Centre (1972–present date). These venues are not Indigenous-specific.

was common in the gay subculture where drag kings and queens rubbed shoulders with crossdressers and transgender people. Jamie Goulet remembers, "They were all crossdressing. We used to have so much fun on Manitoba [Avenue], then the place downstairs on Albert [Street]—it was in the basement; there was a club there [The Detour]." Pruden used to struggle with internalized transphobia: "When I first came to [Winnipeg], I was so disgusted when I seen a man in a dress... when we were at that gay bar.... Those were my thoughts because I had just come off the reserve... Look at me now—I never knew I was going to be living as a full female." Other places on the margins of Winnipeg were also identified as early queer gathering places. Olson and others mention "the Hill" (behind the Legislative building, along the Assiniboine River, down to Bonnycastle Park) where 2SLGBTQ would party, hook up, and turn tricks, often, again, for survival.

2SLGBTQ organizations such as the Nichiwakan Native Gay Society, later the Two-Spirited People of Manitoba (TSPM), and the annual International Two-Spirit Gathering were entry points into queer activism. Over thirty-two years, the International 2S Gathering has been held in eleven US states and seven provinces in Canada. It was held at the Sandy-Saulteaux Spiritual Centre near Beausejour, Manitoba in 1990, 1998, 2010, and 2018.[22] Barbara Bruce has attended the gathering eight times; she says, "That's activism: coming together and talking about culture, and issues that affect us, in a safe place... It provide[s] an opportunity for [2SLGBTQ] people to unite and organize all over North America." These gatherings strengthen 2S identity, self-esteem, and community.

Goulet, Bruce, and Laramee discussed ways in which the 2S movement intersects with the Indigenous women's movement due to shared

22 A 2S elders' council selected Chantal Fiola and Boyd Whiskeyjack as the 2018–2019 International Two-Spirit Ogichidaakwe (Warrior Woman) and Ogichidaa; they represented 2SLGTBQ at cultural events, national expos, and pow wows including the Bay Area American Indian Two-Spirits (BAAITS) Pow Wow in San Francisco, the largest 2S pow wow in the world.

patriarchal oppression, racism, and colonization. Indigenous women's gatherings often provide safe spaces for 2S and trans people to gather. The 2S advocates we spoke with identify Indigenous women allies—such as Goulet's mother, elder Mae Louise Campbell, Leslie Spillett, Linda McEvoy, and the late Barbara Daniels and Velma Orvis—as early advocates for 2SLGBTQ.

2S Activism Over the Years

Reflecting on their long-term 2S activism, the 2S advocates spoke of ongoing involvement in 2SLGBTQ events and organizations, *finding one's place*, 2S advocacy, bringing a 2S perspective into larger Indigenous and queer activism, and the role of Indigenous spirituality.

TSPM became a registered non-profit society in March 2006, and most of the people we spoke with have been involved with this organization for years. TSPM offers regional 2S gatherings, workshops, and fundraises, participates in 2S research, and was instrumental in getting the National Aboriginal Health Organization (NAHO) to publish the 2012 manual "Suicide Prevention and Two-Spirited People."[23] In 2015, McLeod and Merasty met with Perry Bellegarde, National Chief of the AFN, and presented him with three recommendations to support the inclusion of 2S First Nations people. This included the establishment of a national 2S council.

Involvement in the International 2S Gatherings from their inception in 1988 to the present was identified as crucial by everyone (except the 2S youth). These gatherings offer an opportunity for 2S folks to learn about their own culture, language, and ceremonies in safer spaces. There, 2S spiritual leaders, such as Beverly Little Thunder, share nation-specific 2S teachings. Olson discusses the cathartic and healing nature of these gatherings:

23 View the manual here: https://fnim.sehc.com/getmedia/da57be9c-b8bb-4b1d-8250-627d06210871/Suicide_Prevention_2Spirited_People_Guide_2012.pdf.aspx?ext=.

> The Navajo or the Choctaw or the Mi'kmaw, whoever was at that ceremony would learn about [2S people] historically. I was fascinated. What? We [2S] had a role? Roles like taking care of children, orphans, and elders—all the important parts that kept our society together... It felt so good to know that I have 2S ancestors back there who lived a full life without ever being judged. That was the outcome of that [knowledge shared at the gatherings]: our place in the circle, and the term was *debwewin gikendinam.*[24]

In this way, Indigenous culture and ceremony are buffers against systemic homo/transphobia and promote healing.

When recalling their 2S activism, several people spoke of *finding one's place.* Having experienced homo/transphobic discrimination, social stigma, and ostracism, they had to forge their own paths and create their own safe spaces, organizations, and institutions. Pruden remembers, "All of my friends in my circle, the ones that were shunned, would all pull together and we made our own family. There must have been twenty to thirty of us that were together way back in the day, back in the 80s." Similarly, Merasty says, "it was a matter of finding out where you belong, where you felt accepted, whose group you wanted to be a part of." Finding one's place also involves assisting other 2S people, especially youth.

Centering 2S youth is an important aspect of 2S advocacy. Considering all she has survived as a 2S person, Barbara Bruce notes, "I'm so glad I am where I am today and that I can help [2S youth] with anything that they come to me with." As a trans jingle dress dancer, Gayle Pruden travels extensively, making space for younger trans dancers. Sadie-Phoenix Lavoie echoes these themes: "I'm one of you guys and I'm here to learn as much as you. It's a collective process...

24 Olsen directed a National Film Board film in 2008, titled *Second Stories: Deb-we-win Ge-ken-am-aan—Our Place in the Circle,* exploring Indigenous expressions of gender and sexual diversity. Roulette translates this term to "something [truth] we already know." Roulette, personal communication, 2008.

especially with young people. Also learning from older generations and trying to figure out what my place was in the grand scheme of it."

2S advocacy is often connected to larger anti-colonial struggles, and to Indigenous and queer resistance movements.[25] Goulet, McLeod, and Olson link 2S activism to resisting colonization, especially Christian homo/transphobia. McLeod sees the re-introduction of 2S people as spiritually significant beings in Creation as countering church-imposed discrimination. She recognizes this as "our contribution to the queer resistance or human rights movement; we bring back this idea of spirituality." Likewise, Goulet says, "We [2S people] were the ones who had the courage to break through the Eurocentric, patriarchal values that took over all our communities." She connects her 2S activism to the Indigenous women's movement, including raising awareness about domestic violence, and notes a longstanding alliance between Indigenous women allies and 2S people. She explains,

> Whenever there were issues in our communities, those [straight Indigenous] women didn't hesitate on standing up—it was the queer people and them that were able to speak up at that time. And then our trans men, brothers, that were gay or Two-Spirited that would come with us ... [We were pushing the chiefs to be accountable.] The chiefs had to do something about the violence, and even some of them were violent. We were calling them out.

McLeod connects the 2S movement and the arrival of the spiritual name *Two-Spirit* in 1990 with the Oka crisis and the Indigenous-led rejection of the Meech Lake Accord.

Greatest Challenges

The 2S advocates highlighted many challenges throughout their activism, especially within Indigenous communities and ceremonies,

25 Mainstream local and national queer activism are highlighted by Korinek in her *Prairie Fairies*; however, settler colonialism remains undiscussed.

confronting colonization, a lack of safe spaces and resources for 2S youth, suicide and addiction, and challenges within ourselves.[26]

The 2S advocates raised the issue of lateral violence on First Nation reserves in connection to domestic violence, MMIWG2S, and homo/transphobia by authority figures, peer groups, and family. McLeod notes, "There are virulent homo/transphobes in places of power and privilege who still act out." Olson discussed homophobia on reserve and pressure to perform an "appropriate" gender, which grew more serious and violent with age. Upon becoming increasingly feminine around puberty, Olson explains that boys on the reserve would "come to my place to torture me... They were particularly mean to any of the girls that were a little more butch or boys who were more feminine." Merasty does not think the chief and council listen to 2SLGBTQ community members. In 2019, McLeod was invited to speak at Cross Lake First Nation's first Pride event, but her flight was "sabotaged." Lavoie discussed misconceptions and stereotypes about 2S people and homophobic teasing in Sagkeeng First Nation[27] and the difficulty of being active in 2S resurgence on reserve after moving to Winnipeg.

Colonial complacency is another challenge. After thirty years of activism, McLeod is frustrated by "people sitting back who should be activists, or letting other people do all the work and then benefitting from it." Lavoie highlights superficial support by institutions, corporations, and Pride Winnipeg. Exposing tepid support from universities, they explain, "you can only hide behind gender-neutral washrooms for so long... How are we respecting our 2S faculty and students?" Administrators who give greetings at 2S events then leave immediately cannot hear what the 2S community is saying. A checklist for social responsibility without follow-through maintains heteronormative white supremacy, including in the mainstream LGBTQ community. Lavoie has quit "trying to brown up that space... It's draining and

26 Other challenges included trans rights in prison, sexual reassignment surgery access and wait times, and trans/homophobia in Christianity.

27 They also mentioned efforts by chief and council and the school to correct this.

exhausting having to do the labour of educating them," and focuses instead on 2SQTPOC spaces.

Lack of resources for 2S youth, suicide, addiction, and internal struggles were also raised as ongoing challenges. Pruden and Merasty note that bars are inappropriate for 2S youth because of age restrictions, addictions, and hypersexualization. Pruden believes the biggest challenge for 2S youth today is meth addiction and longs for a safe house (and transportation) where 2S/trans youth can hang out sober, connect with 2S elders, and not get kicked out after a couple of hours. Olson and McLeod link these issues to suicide and a lack of support in 2S people's families and home communities. Some note challenges within oneself; for example, Lavoie feels they should have come out sooner and works not to let fear control their actions when faced with adversity. Laramee encourages 2S folks to understand who we are and offers her mother's advice: "*Niibawi*, stand up, and be the best [2S person] you can be."

2S Resurgence Grounded in Indigenous Spirituality

Indigenous ceremonies for well-being are part of 2S resurgence. Unfortunately, challenges—including colonial dogma regulating clothing and Indigenous women and 2SLGBTQ bodies—are also found therein. Nonetheless, the importance of Indigenous spirituality and 2S ceremonies are paramount.

Christianity devastated Indigenous spirituality, gender, and sexual diversity, debased Indigenous women and 2S authority, and presented Creator as male only and Creation as male dominant. According to Goulet, "Eurocentric patriarchy has flooded our ceremonies" and "eradicated our matriarchal governance system and that sacred feminine principle that drove our people." Laramee's family carries stories about the criminalization of Indigenous ceremonies in Canada and how people adapted: "The men took the [ceremonial] bundles to the bush, and the women took the children to the church because that was the only legal way to have prayers in our house... That's how women got separated from ceremonies." Bruce discussed the resulting gender imbalance in ceremonial leadership, the importance of grandmothers and matriarchs leading ceremony, and the importance of remembering *Gizhe-Manidokwe* (Creator as female). Lavoie identifies ceremony as the site of greatest resistance to them as a 2S genderfluid person.

Everyone we spoke with has experienced homo/transphobia and lateral violence in ceremony. When Laramee's sexuality became known in the local Midewiwin lodge, she suffered homophobic ostracism that kept her away from ceremonies for *fourteen years*! At age fifteen, Olson travelled to Wisconsin and approached the leader of a Midewiwin survival school seeking admission. Olson remembers that the leader "wouldn't even make eye contact with me... He made homophobic jokes... to let me know that he knows that I was gay, and he wasn't interested in having me in his school." This scarred Olson; he avoided ceremonies for five years.

Christian gender dichotomy and dogma regarding "appropriate" gendered clothing is difficult for many 2S people. Skirts are often forced or forbidden depending on perceived gender identity. Lavoie spoke of being "attacked" by elders in a pipe ceremony for not wearing a skirt and becoming fearful of attending ceremony without one. Pruden experienced transphobic remarks while wearing women's pow wow regalia, including comments about having "big hands and feet *for a woman*." The 2S advocates also highlighted taboos around menstruation and fear of persecution for 2S advocacy.

2S resistance and agency are also found in a ceremonial context. Upon returning to ceremonies, Olson questioned spiritual leadership about Creation stories featuring 2S people; he points out, however, that there has been progress in the Mide society because leaders had 2S daughters. Similarly, Lavoie questions Sundance leadership and their ability to ensure it is a safe space for 2S people; they have pushed for acceptance of gender and sexual diversity and were recently permitted to participate in a male-only ceremony.

Two-Spirit ceremonies, lodges, leadership, elders, conductors, and helpers are vital. Ceremonies have strengthened Merasty's "belief in Creator, creation, 2S people and what they're capable of, how powerful they are...They belong in the ceremonies." Bruce recognizes 2S people are gifted despite our persecution. Goulet hopes to speak with 2S elders regarding 2S roles and clothing/regalia and to share this with other 2S people. She insists this guidance must "come from us [as 2S people] not a male elder telling us [about] 2S people." Likewise, McLeod explains,

> We created our own [spiritual] community in the absence, or because of a traumatized colonial one that would not accept us. We have our [own 2S] elders...We've been doing our own sweat lodges and pipe ceremonies, gathering our medicines, giving our own teachings, having and raising our own children, doing our own Sundance, digging our own pipestone.

Bruce notes a 2S Midewiwin chief (in Ontario), a 2S Sundance chief (in the US), and 2S sweat lodge conductors (including herself, Laramee, and McLeod) as among this spiritual community. Pruden knows someone who is being mentored to raise a 2S Sundance lodge.[28] Lavoie talked about the *Rainbow Warriors*, a new organization of 2S youth in Winnipeg who often approach 2S elders for ceremonies. The (drug- and alcohol-free) International 2S Gatherings host ceremonies and are transformational for many people. Lorne notes these gatherings "might be the only time they ever experience being sober because they feel safe enough to put their addictions aside just to experience it."[29] 2S advocates are making promising gains in a ceremonial context.

28 In another example, in 2022, 2Spirit Manitoba purchased land an hour outside Winnipeg with the intention of hosting 2S ceremonies. To date, they have hosted 2S sweat lodges, a 2S fasting camp, and plans are underway to host the first 2S Sundance in the summer of 2023 with 2S and trans Métis elder, Charlotte Nolin, as the Sundance chief, and 2S elders Barbara Bruce and Albert McLeod also playing leadership roles.

29 These 2S advocates often raised the importance of sobriety in their lives.

On the Horizon for 2S Resurgence

Improvements in the lives of 2S people are noticeable today. McLeod shares, "It was our dream way back when, in our years of segregation and isolation, that we would have our own safer, sacred space, and now we're on the verge of it being real." Merasty says, "the further we go into the future, the better it'll get because we're not fighting the same battle over and over." According to Olson, as 2S people remember our "place in the circle," the younger generation will only know "this is where we fit in. They don't have to know the last two centuries of what was put upon us." Lavoie spoke of 2S youth "living their best life" earlier these days. Conversely, everyone also identified outstanding 2S needs.

Unlearning harmful Eurocentric and patriarchal ways, especially in our Indigenous governments, institutions, organizations, communities, and spirituality is critical. Pruden insists that heteronormativity must no longer be forced in ceremonies (or anywhere). Goulet identified the inappropriateness of straight, cisgender elders reprimanding 2S people. Goulet and Olson spoke of 2S people taking back our ceremonies and being welcomed back into spiritual societies. Goulet, Lavoie, and Bruce connected the re-emergence of matriarchal teachings with 2S resurgence to promote Indigenous women's and 2SLGBTQ authority.

Efforts by allies are welcome, but, ultimately, it is time for 2S people to be supported to provide for our own needs. McLeod believes we need "our own 2S organizations providing services to other 2S people. We're now in a position to access resources to make that possible in the next ten years." He spoke of the creation of 2S institutions such as education, health, housing, and leadership. Olson and Merasty highlighted the need for all areas of society to engage in these pursuits, and to stop treating 2S folks as an afterthought. Laramee and Lavoie encourage us to focus on and privilege 2SBIPOC relationships, elders, and youth. 2S organizations like the national 2SinMotion, the provincial 2Spirit Manitoba, and the Two-Spirit Michif Local in Winnipeg can facilitate such endeavours.

While improvements in the lives of 2S people are recognized, much work remains to decolonize our nations. Two-Spirit people must take the lead in identifying our own needs and potential solutions—we must be adequately resourced and supported in this.

What We've Learned

The 2S advocates featured in this chapter carry a wealth of 2S knowledge. Without fanfare or recognition, they have dedicated themselves to bettering the lives of 2SLGBTQ people and contributed to the development and maintenance of Indigenous 2S organizations like the Nichiwakan Native Gay Society, Two-Spirited People of Manitoba, and the Two-Spirit Michif Local in Winnipeg. Their participation in mainstream LGBTQ organizations, especially social clubs and lounges like Gio's, Happenings, and Ms. Purdy's, enabled these to be some of the longest-running queer spaces in Canada.[30]

These 2S advocates began their participation in the 2S movement out of necessity and survival; several did not think of their efforts as "activism" or "resistance." Their loved ones were dying from HIV/AIDS, addictions, and suicide; immediate advocacy and action were needed, so they stepped up. Two-Spirit people carry colonial trauma from racism, sexism, and homo/transphobia; however, we also carry resilience and the sacred bundles of our people.

Indigenous cultures, languages, and spirituality offer buffers against homo/transphobia and 2S erasure in their recognition of animate and inanimate distinctions in Creation, and in their recognition of diverse genders and sexualities. Collectively untangling colonialism, the 2S advocates take solace in knowing that 2S people are sacred. 2S people are rediscovering nation-specific 2S teachings and ceremonies and recognizing that being 2S is a gift from Creator. While ceremonies are a grounding force for 2S resurgence, 2S people themselves are needed to heal, balance, and decolonize Indigenous nations.

30 Korinek, *Prairie Fairies*, 156-157.

2S resurgence contributes to the reclamation of Indigenous sovereignty. Two-Spirit people have opened doors, made spaces, and identified a path forward for themselves. We created family and community when we were excluded from our own. We have made significant gains so that 2S youth do not have to fight all the same battles. According to Lavoie, "The [2S] kids are starting to feel safer and embracing themselves [sooner]...They have agency to advocate and that if they see something that they want then they should strive for it." In the ongoing work of healing ourselves as 2SLGBTQ, we are also helping heal our organizations, home communities, and nations, as well as non-Indigenous institutions.

We say *miigwetch, ekosani, marsii, thank you* to Barbara Bruce, Myra Laramee, Jamie Goulet, Connie Merasty, Lorne Olson, Sadie-Phoenix Lavoie, Albert McLeod, and Gayle Pruden, for sharing their experiences and for their ongoing 2SLGBTQ advocacy. We invite others to learn more about the rich history of 2S reclamation, organizations, activism, and resistance that has been occurring in Winnipeg (and beyond) for the last half-century (and earlier). We encourage 2SLGBTQ readers (and allies) to follow in the footsteps of these advocates and contribute to 2SLGBTQ resurgence.

Bibliography

Brayboy, Duane. "Two-Spirits, One Heart, Five Genders." *Indian Country Today Media Network*, January 23, 2016. http://indiancountrytodaymedianetwork.com/2016/01/23/two-spirits-one-heart-five-genders.

Chambers, Stuart. "Pierre Elliott Trudeau and Bill C-150: A Rational Approach to Homosexual Acts, 1968–69." *Journal of Homosexuality* 57, 2 (2010): 249–266.

C2C. *The Findings of C2C: Two Spirit & Queer/Trans People of Colour; Calls to Action 2019*. Conference findings from C2C: Two-Spirit & Queer/Trans People of Colour, the University of Winnipeg, Winnipeg, MB, October 20–22, 2017, Chantal Fiola and Sharanpal Ruprai, co-chairs, 2019. https://www.uwinnipeg.ca/c2c/docs/c2c_calls-to-action_final.pdf.

Eskridge, William. *Dishonorable Passions: Sodomy Laws in America, 1861–2003*. Toronto: Penguin Group, 2008.

Fiola, Chantal. "Naawenangweyaabeg Coming In: Intersections of Indigenous Sexuality and Spirituality." In *In Good Relation: History, Gender, and Kinship in Indigenous Feminisms*, edited by Sarah Nickel and Amanda Fehr, 136–153. Winnipeg: University of Manitoba Press, 2020.

Floresco, Aaron, dir. *One Gay City: A History of LGBT Life in Winnipeg*. Winnipeg: Past Perfect Productions, 2014. DVD.

Garvin, John, ed. "Charles Mair," in *Canadian Poets*. Toronto: McClelland, Goodchild and Steward, 1916: 19-32.

Jacobs, Sue-Ellen, Wesley Thomas, and Sabine Lang. *Two-Spirit People: Native American Gender Identity, Sexuality, and Spirituality*. Chicago: University of Illinois Press, 1997.

Korinek, Valerie. *Prairie Fairies: A History of Queer Communities and People in Western Canada, 1930–1985*. Toronto: University of Toronto Press, 2018.

Korinek, Valerie. "'We're the Girls of the Pansy Parade': Historicizing Winnipeg's Queer Subcultures, 1930s–1970." *Social History* 45, no. 89 (2012): 117–155.

National Aboriginal Health Organization (NAHO). 2012. Suicide Prevention and Two-Spirited People. https://fnim.sehc.com/getmedia/da57be9c-b8bb-4b1d-8250-627d06210871/Suicide_Prevention_2Spirited_People_Guide_2012.pdf.aspx?ext=.pdf.

Olsen, Lorne, dir., *Second Stories: Deb-we-win Ge-ken-am-aan—Our Place in the Circle*. National Film Board of Canada, 2008.

Pyle, Kai. "We Were There Too! Queer, Trans, and 2Spirit Métis History," 5 May 2022. Mawachihitotaak Métis Studies Symposium, 3-6 May 2022. Hybrid Zoom & Winnipeg, MB.

Roulette, Roger. Personal communication. 2008.

Roulette, Roger. Personal communication. 2017.

Trudeau, Justin. "Remarks by Prime Minster Justin Trudeau to Apologize to LGBTQ2 Canadians." Prime Minster of Canada Justin Trudeau. November 28, 2017. https://pm.gc.ca/en/news/speeches/2017/11/28/remarks-prime-minister-justin-trudeau-apologize-lgbtq2-canadians.

"Two-Spirit Archives." The University of Winnipeg. Accessed December 26, 2022. https://archives.uwinnipeg.ca/our-collections/two-spirit-archives.html.

Wilson, Alex. "N'tacimowin inna nah': Our Coming in Stories." *Canadian Woman Studies* 26, no. 3–4 (2008): 193–199. http://cws.journals.yorku.ca/index.php/cws/article/viewFile/22131/20785.

Kathy Mallett is a member of the Fisher River Cree Nation and was born and raised in Winnipeg. Kathy attended schools in the inner city of Winnipeg. She has a history degree from the University of Winnipeg. She has been involved in the Aboriginal community for well over 40 years. Her involved in various issues dealing with education, housing, violence against women, child welfare, international development, community and economic development. Currently, Kathy is on the board of Reconciliation Thunder and a community member on the Manitoba Research Alliance.

Kathy's first community recognition came when she received in 1985 YWCA Woman of the Year in Community Service. She also received in 2011 the Order of Manitoba (O.M), and in the same year was inducted in Kanikanichihk's 12the Annual "Keeping the Fires Burning." Lastly, in 2015 Kathy was recognized by the Errol Black Chair in Labour Issues from the Canadian Centre for Policy Alternatives—Manitoba office.

Dr. Shauna MacKinnon is Professor and Chair, Department of Urban and Inner-City Studies at the University of Winnipeg, situated at Merchants Corner in Winnipeg's North End. Dr. Mackinnon has conducted numerous studies related to public policy, poverty and inequality, typically utilizing a collaborative, community based research approach. She is author of *Decolonizing Employment: Aboriginal Inclusion in the Labour Market* (2015) and editor of *Practising Community Based Participatory Research Stories: Stories of Engagement, Empowerment, and Mobilization* (2018). Dr. MacKinnon has been involved with the Manitoba Research Alliance (MRA) since 2003. In 2020, the MRA was awarded a 7-year, $2.5 million Social Science Humanities Research Council (SSHRC) Partnership Grant for the community driven "Solutions to Poverty: Challenges and Possibilities" project. She succeeded her friend and mentor, Dr. John Loxley, as the Principal Investigator of the MRA after his passing in 2020. In addition to her academic work, MacKinnon is actively engaged in community-led social justice initiatives and political advocacy.